The Lost Art of
Romance

How to Romance a Lady

By
Richard Connelly

Order this book online at www.trafford.com
or email orders@trafford.com

Most Trafford titles are also available at major online book retailers.

Note for Librarians: A cataloguing record for this book is available from Library
and Archives Canada at www.collectionscanada.ca/amicus/index-e.html

Printed in Victoria, BC, Canada.

ISBN: 978-1-4269-1406-5 (soft cover)
ISBN: 978-1-4269-1407-2 (hard cover)

Library of Congress Control Number: 2009932573

*Our mission is to efficiently provide the world's finest, most comprehensive
book publishing service, enabling every author to experience success.
To find out how to publish your book, your way, and have it available
worldwide, visit us online at www.trafford.com*

Trafford rev. 08/18/09

www.trafford.com

North America & international
toll-free: 1 888 232 4444 (USA & Canada)
phone: 250 383 6864 ♦ fax: 812 355 4082

The Lost Art of
Romance

Dedicated To

All of the Numerous Ladies Who Assisted Me
The Guys from my Prison Ministry
and
To
My Dancing Jeanie

Contents

Preface

Why this book?

Where I live, unofficial statistics indicate that 4 out of 5 divorces are filed by women. So, does this suggest something about women or does it point to faults in us men? The culture of today, specifically television and media commercials, portrays men as ignorant, lazy, uncouth slobs. Just sit and watch network television for one evening and you will see a wide variety of intelligent, caring women in comic farces trying to deal with the slovenly, unfeeling men in their lives. Most commercials portray males in a similar fashion during the breaks.

While I do not believe this to be an accurate assessment of most men, the old expression, "Where there is smoke, there is fire," does apply to some degree. I am not here to place blame or argue as to who or what is responsible for the 50% divorce rate in the U.S.

I experienced a divorce some 8 years ago. For many years I considered her to be mostly at fault. After all, how could a kind, intelligent, cultured and hard working man like myself be to blame? Do you detect some of my male ego peeking through? Most of us men have an abundance of it. In fact, the male ego is in part what makes us men...the hard charging, confident working man and provider. (Women love a man who is confident, but not arrogant...a fine line sometimes.)

I have also written a book entitled **What Men Really Think of Women By a Few Good Men**. Don't go looking for it on the shelves. (My ex wife who read part of the previous book would be shocked to know of this book.) This previous literary effort on my part was far from being complimentary about the female of our species. I have, however, had an epiphany or shall we say a change of heart. To paraphrase the Bible, "You must remove the log from your own eye before you can see clearly to remove the speck from someone else's eye".

I sense that many women today are cynical about men, dislike our foibles, and have little respect for males. During the women's liberation movement of the 1960's and 1970's, we men were conditioned to not offer seats on a bus, not open doors for a woman, etc. I truly believe, however, that much of this liberation movement was about equal pay for equal work, equality of opportunity, and many more good things which women both wanted and deserve. I am all for it.

Unfortunately, as with any radical social change, there are many times when a passion for a cause takes it to extremes. Men and women are different. Many books have described these differences in how we think and how we process information and emotions. The differences exist, and whether or not you believe in God or evolution, or whatever, I believe that these differences are complimentary although they frequently seem antagonistic.

I have conducted countless, unscientific and informal interviews with many women of all ages for this book. I have heard mostly that ladies do wish for a return to manners, chivalry, romance, and respect from men. I have also spoken with many men who surprisingly enough offered many ideas on romance that were not mentioned by ladies. Especially rare was the idea of romance for young women. I frequently heard comments from them like "Young men don't do romance any more" or from one obviously jaded, young woman, "The most romantic thing my man has done for me is pay the bills on time". I find this sad. There appears to be one or more generations for which romance is dead or at least with one foot in the grave. So I hope that this book might be a humble attempt to revive romance for some couples and instill it in young men who seem to know little about it.

This book is not about relationships between men and women. I have no qualifications or psychological training which would allow me to address this issue. I will leave this to Oprah and Dr. Phil. What I do have is deep thought on the idea of romance, a school of hard knocks, and countless interviews and observations from which to offer these ideas and suggestions on how to romance a lady. And I do mean "lady".

In the conventional sense of the words all men are not "gentlemen," just as all women are not "ladies". I do not wish to infer any kind of social level or economic status through the use of the term lady. I sense that most, if not all, women want to be considered as ladies. I also believe that, due to their interactions with men, many are not ladies. Again I am not assigning blame. It could be said that the definition of a lady is a woman who allows or demands that a man act like a gentleman.

Remember the Biblical statement about the log in the eye? This is a book about us men first removing that log from our eye. We have to clean up our own act first. We must undertake the task of romancing the women in our lives, whether or not it is a first date or our 50th wedding anniversary. Let us see clearly to turning women into ladies and ladies into women who are happy and fully satisfied with the love of their life.

Foreward

As stated in the preface, this is not a book about relationships between men and women. It is rather a simple "How to" book which offers some suggestions on romantic things you can do for a lady in your life. It applies to all stages of a relationship from first date onwards.

If you have purchased this book because you are having deep difficulties with your lady and your relationship is much less than what it should be, then I highly recommend that you go get a refund and purchase instead the book, **The Love Dare**, from the movie **Fireproof**. That is the book you need right now to get your relationship back on solid ground. After applying the techniques found in **The Love Dare** book, I would highly recommend that you see the movie **Fireproof** with your lady. The movie is about a fire chief (played by Kirk Cameron) who is facing a divorce from his wife. In the movie the man's father asks him to delay the divorce for 40 days and gives him a book called **The Love Dare** to read and do what it says to do. The book explains the nature of true love and gives the reader a specific and different task to do for each of 40 days for their spouse. This book is now for sale at most book stores. **The Love Dare** will get the fire in your relationship started again and then read **The Lost Art of Romance** to keep the sparks flying.

The movie **Fireproof** and the book **The Love Dare** are Christian based, and I understand that you may not be a believer. It matters not, for the principles are solid and the things this book tells you to do, work. I am not attempting in this book to preach at you or convert you to any specific set of beliefs. The ideas contained herein are only suggestions and a potential guide for doing certain romantic tasks correctly.

In John Eldredge's **Wild at Heart**, (another book I highly recommend that all men read) the author indicates that there are three things a man wishes to do in his life: Fight a battle, live an adventure, and rescue a beauty. This is the essence of a man. There is beauty in every woman. The beauty may not be physical, but there can be beauty in the heart and soul of a woman if the right man comes along to bring it forth.

Having been raised in New Orleans I love raw oysters. It is, however, the taste I crave. Sitting there on the shells, they actually look like something expelled from the chest or nose of a person with a terrible cold or bronchitis. Not beautiful to look at and, for many, a terrible thing to taste, but I love them. The raw oyster can also frequently contain one of nature's most beautiful objects, the pearl. In all women, beauty can be found. Read some of the **Songs of Solomon** from the Bible to truly experience beauty and a deep passionate love that can spring from almost any woman.

In the book, **The Love Dare**, we are admonished to be patient, kind, unselfish, and thoughtful when dealing with our ladies. It paraphrases a passage from the New Testament, first Corinthians, chapter 13, verses 4 through 7 which says:

Love suffers long and is kind
love does not envy
love does not parade itself
is not puffed up
does not behave rudely
does not seek its own
is not provoked
thinks no evil
does not rejoice in iniquity
but rejoices in the truth
bears all things
believes all things
hopes all things
endures all things.*

* New King James Version

Seek out the true and deeper meaning of these principles when dealing with a woman, or for that matter virtually any human being you interact with; be they woman or man. **The Love Dare** book explains these principles very well.

My book, meaning this book, is not a sex manual. Good romance can obviously lead to a sex event, and I touch on certain things which may be done in or out of the bedroom. There is, however, a lot of advice for good sex which has been published, and whether good advice or not, it can also be found in the check out line at your neighborhood grocery store. It is hoped that sex is performed in the context of a marriage or a truly committed and loving relationship, but I am not making that distinction. Many of the ideas in this book are designed for a first date, which is hopefully not a one night stand.

The most important aspect I can relate in this book is the need for unconditional love when dealing with your lady. Do not ever consider doing some of the romantic ideas contained herein with the motivation of receiving sex from a woman or any other reward in return. While it is very conceivable that your lady may wish to "jump your bones", shower you with kisses, or show her appreciation in many ways after you have performed some of the tasks herein, your motivation for doing them will ultimately be apparent to her. Let her know that you expect nothing in return, that you are merely doing something nice and/or loving for her and you may indeed be surprised at the return you get.

For women who read this book, many of you will not agree with everything I say. In truth many of the women who reviewed portions of the book did not agree with every statement. In the case of dissenting opinions, I gravitated toward the majority view. At one point I was allowing a young married couple to review the "Basics" chapter and about every few minutes she was stabbing her finger at an idea and glaring at her husband. I quickly grabbed the manuscript back not wishing to cause the poor young man grief.

If you are a woman reading this book please be kind in presenting it to your man. As the author, I do not claim to follow all of the principles contained herein. I try, but fall short on a frequent basis. I suggest that you ladies also read Steve Harvey's book **Act Like a Lady...Think Like a Man**. This book will give you considerable insight into the nature of men and why we act as we do. Hopefully, Harvey's book will also show you ladies the nature of the power that you have over men.

There are several parts to this book. Chapter One attempts to define romance, while Chapter Two deals with what I call the "Basics" or the courtesies that every man should extend to every lady from day one of their relationship to death do you part. Other chapters deal with romantic ideas or fun and unusual dates. If a particular romantic idea requires some detail then I expand upon it. Details are important. If you are going to do something nice for your lady, then by all means do it right. Use these chapters as a check list.

You may also just review the extensive table of contents and find an idea which appeals to you or more importantly an idea which you think your lady will enjoy. Many of the ideas may require a considerable expenditure of funds on your part, but most can be accomplished with just your time and effort. Never forget that small gestures of affection and romance done frequently can greatly outweigh the large single event done seldomly.

Many will call me a dinosaur for the sentiments and gestures expressed herein. Well, **mea culpa**, I am guilty. I am both an older guy and an old fashioned guy, who firmly believes that more romance by men toward their ladies will benefit both. I know that both young men and young women may laugh at some of the ideas herein. Okay laugh away, but...

ROMANCE YOUR LADY EVERY DAY!

What is Romance?

Let us men ask ourselves: what is romance? Do we really know what the term means? Likely we think we do, but many women say we have no clue. **Wikipedia** on line defines romance as: "a. A love affair, b. Ardent emotional attachment or involvement between people; love." Romance also describes some forms of literature, music and art.

As a lost art, we men need to rediscover the artful form of romancing a woman. When interviewing both men and women for this book I asked many to define the word as if they were writing a definition for the dictionary. Most men were unable to do so, but surprisingly enough many women were also unsure as to a workable definition. I would suggest that most women know it when they see it, and furthermore, many ladies are fascinated by the concept. It is my understanding that the worldwide distribution of romance novels is a business worth billions in retail sales. I have also heard that television daytime soap operas produce the profits which allow for the production of the more expensive nighttime shows which typically do not make a profit. Women do tend to speak of relationships among themselves in serious terms. It is not the more common "locker room" talk in which men often engage.

Romance is indeed an art form. It should be studied and practiced. As every woman is an individual human being, each will have her own preferences. Seek them out. Even the process of discovery can be a romantic adventure in and of itself. Practice can make it perfect!

I will not bore you with the many answers I received from both men and women when asked to define romance. I will, however, give you one which I received very early on and still seems to be the most appropriate. This came from a woman named Jenny who simply stated that romance from a man is "making her smile", and there is nothing more beautiful and bright as a smile from your lady when directed at you.

Discerning the term romance may be as difficult as defining love. Writers and poets have attempted to describe and quantify love for centuries with varying degrees of success. Most of us know the feeling of love when cupid slings his arrows our way, and that first flush of deep feelings you have for a lady are difficult to fathom. Unfortunately the deep infatuation and longing that first come with an unbridled passion for a woman may soon fade as familiarity and comfort grow. I think this is best. It is hard to imagine living for the rest of your life with the excitement and lust that come with a new love or first love. The human species would be very unproductive indeed were we to keep this passion throughout the years. It would be nice, but hardly practical.

I am speaking as a man, and most men have responsibilities to work, provide and protect those whom we love, as women have equally important tasks of their own. In **The Love Dare** book, the authors speak of love as a choice we may make following the overwhelming early stages of love. We choose to love someone when the deep feelings have tempered in their intensity. Romancing your lady is a choice you can make.

I do not pretend in any manner to understand the depths of a woman's heart, but I believe that certain observations can be made. I know much of what follows may be offensive to some women. You have my apologies if you are offended, but what I say is not meant to be derogatory, but complimentary, and this book is truly intended for men.

Many little girls are raised on the **Cinderella** concept. Most will have seen the Walt Disney movie very early in their lives and are thus indoctrinated with the idea of a **Prince Charming** sweeping

2

them off their feet to live happily ever after. Indeed their mothers want them to marry this **Prince Charming** and often groom them to do so. After all, the mother failed to marry the prince, and both men and women often relive their lives vicariously through their children and want the very best for them. Dad wants the son to score the touchdown now that he is too old to do so. This is natural. Unfortunately, none of us men are or will ever be a prince, but we might learn to be charming and romantic. It is also possible, however, that a man can become this prince for his lady, at least in her mind. Most women, by design, are nurturing and love the very notion of love and hence romance.

I am no expert in love, having been "in love" only a limited number of times, but my observations tell me that a woman's love for a man is more giving, more passionate, more unconditional, and stronger than most men are capable of experiencing. Steve Harvey says it well in his book **Act Like a Lady – Think Like a Man**. We men have three issues with which we express love. Profess, provide and protect. Read his book for an explanation. Mr. Harvey does, however, examine an overriding issue which initiates and causes a continuation of the courting of a woman by a man. The "Cookie". This is what the woman possesses and the man wants. He contends that this cookie is what causes a man to begin talking to a strange woman and what he is seeking in an initial encounter. I will not dispute Mr. Harvey, and it is hoped that you understand what he means by the "Cookie".

Most women understand this is what the man is seeking, but tend to ignore the fact with their **Cinderella** mindset. I would, therefore, ask men to look deeper into a woman's character, soul and mind. Having experienced the "one night stand" in my youth, I would ask all men to honestly evaluate the experience. Did it leave you feeling as empty as I felt? Were the hours of effort worth the 8 seconds? In my experience making love is much more fulfilling than just having sex.

When dating, in both love and sex a woman is giving of herself to the man. A man is merely in a position to take from her and sometimes justifies it with a dinner and a movie, or a few drinks at the bar. Do not take from a lady. What she gives means more to her heart and soul than the brief pleasure you have in the taking. It has been said that men trade affection for sex, while a woman trades sex for affection. This is not to say that sex is not important to woman. A recent scientific study indicates that a woman in orgasm almost totally blocks all other sensory inputs to her brain while a man does not. There is great intensity in sex for a woman, but it appears to be as much or more mental than it is physical. Romance is a huge part of the mental, and she will need it all of her life.

Love your lady before you take from her.

Romance your lady with sincerity, with passion, and with your heart, and she will give more than you could ever imagine taking.

Basics…

The basics for romancing a woman…

The following are standard courtesies which should be employed by the man on a date with a woman or in a relationship. Some are appropriate for the first date and some are more typical of a long term relationship or in marriage. Obviously in a long term relationship most gentlemen will begin to slide on many of the items listed below. Indeed, some ladies with whom I consulted, thought I should group these items by first date, long term dating, etc.

I have, however, chosen not to do so. For one, trying to decide which is a first date effort only is by far too difficult and may raise objections from some readers, and secondly I sincerely believe that all of these items are important for turning a first date into a second date, a second date into a committed relationship, a relationship into a marriage, and a marriage into the sustainable and lifetime pledge that it was always intended to be.

Call this section a stream of consciousness on my part. You may need to read it several times. There will be more basics offered through out this book.

- Always open doors for her, including a car door
- When opening a car door for a lady always look away. The skirt she has on may make it difficult for her to enter or exit a vehicle in a modest manner.
- Always check to see that a woman's dress in inside the vehicle before closing the door.
- Always rise when she rises from a table or returns to it
- Hold and help adjust her chair when you seat her

- Always help a lady with her coat, both on and off.
- Teach your male children, if any, to show manners to their mother by opening doors and waiting for her to enter first. Teach them all of the common manners and they will reflect well on both you and her.
- Just as you would with any friend, use the lady's name frequently in conversation. People like hearing their name. Using it frequently might also prevent you from using another woman's name at a future inopportune time which could instantly kill the relationship.
- Do not use profanity in the presence of a lady or tell off color jokes. After all you want her to be a "lady" so treat her like one. Profane language in a man often indicates a lack of intelligence or thoughtful articulation.
- Always offer your coat if she is cold.
- In the early stages of a relationship do not call a lady frequently at her place of work. At the least it could be embarrassing to her (She may not have a private office), and at the most it could get her fired.
- Assume she will be late when picking her up for a date so schedule the pick up time accordingly and do not show impatience. (My apologies to those ladies who are on time) Acting impatient will likely just slow her down. If there is an event that you need to be on time for, then schedule backwards from the time of the event and add at least 15 minutes for contingency and make that the time you will pick her up. For example; If a concert starts at 7:00 PM, it takes 30 minutes to get there, you allow 15 minutes for possible traffic, then tell your lady you will pick her up at 6:00 PM. You do not want a date to start with stress.
- Always call a lady if you are going to be late picking her up for a date. Even five minutes late… call her!
- Do not take a lady on a date to a smoking venue if she does not smoke. It will, at the very least, annoy her and make her clothes smell. At worst it could make her ill.

- Your first movie date with a lady should be a romantic comedy, not a slasher flick or one with nudity or profane language. It could embarrass her and ruin any rapport between you.
- When asking a woman out for a date try to indicate the form of dress which will be appropriate, but do not be specific. (i.e. do not tell her to wear a skirt or slacks or the length of the skirt, etc.) Allow her to question you about the venue. (The best thing to do is tell her what you will be wearing and she can take her cue from your intended outfit.)
- Always be clean, well groomed, closely shaved, appropriately dressed, and neat in appearance for a date, whether or not it is the first date or 1000th. Dress to the level you told her about and do not deviate. Clip any nose or ear hair, shine your shoes, and spend more than $12.00 on your haircut. Ladies notice the efforts you put into your appearance and appreciate it.
- Do not correct your lady, especially in public. She may quote a statistic wrong, state that the capital of Texas is Houston (it's Austin), or ask if there are extra innings in a football game. Let it slide! It is more important to the future of your relationship to ignore a wrongful statement than it is to correct her in front of others. They may correct her, but you should not. This is, of course, not meant to suggest that if she is about to run a red light that you remain silent. (It happens to both men and women, ladies...no suggestion or implied thought on lack of feminine driving abilities).
- When walking down a sidewalk always position yourself on the outside/traffic side. It may protect her from a splash, indicates a level of protection you are extending to her, and also allows her to view any articles of interest in the passing shops. (You can get some good ideas about future gifts)
- Always call her following a date the **very** next day in order to show interest and tell her that you enjoyed the previous time with her, unless, of course, you did not enjoy the date. While

some ladies have told me three days is acceptable, I tend to disagree. If you liked her call her immediately. If you fail to call her the next day and she likes you, you will cause her undue stress for the next few days worrying about whether or not you liked her. Be kind and save her this possible stress. Call her!

- If you find that you have been thinking about your lady lately, call her and say so. You never know when getting that call will brighten up a rough day for her. It will also make her feel like she is special to you.

- Always defend your lady and her honor in public. It is hoped that a need for violence does not arise, but if it does, it is further hoped that you can be a peacemaker. (A woman may need an energetic defense from you but is typically more embarrassed should a public brawl occur). Defend her verbally at all times and do not allow any man to make fun of her or make unwarranted and unwanted advances. However, be prepared to defend. If you can not honestly say to yourself that you are willing to defend her with your life, should the unlikely occurrence arise, then do not ask her out for a date. She is your responsibility.

- Always remember important dates (i.e. Her birthday, etc.). I suggest that you use your computer to remind you of important dates or else prepare a calendar at the beginning of the year with all important dates noted.

- When on a dinner date, give her an idea of what you intend to order from the menu. Most polite ladies will tend to order a meal of equivalent cost and usually will also order less than what they truly desire, so following her main order, proceed to add on some appetizers which she will enjoy. Do not skimp or be cheap. If there are leftovers then leave it for the first few dates. Suggest a "doggy bag" only on future dates. **What is a man's idea of a gourmet restaurant?** Someplace without a drive up window!

- If you should request a "doggie bag" at a restaurant (Never do this on the first few dates), then carry it out yourself. Do not allow the lady to carry it.
- Speaking of doggies, try to love your lady's pets as well as her. A pet might be the most significant entity in her life... yes even more important than you. I once dated a woman who had a Dachshund, which lunged at my face and tried always to bite me. I just waited for my lady to leave the room once and me and the dog had a "Come to Jesus" meeting. Now before anyone accuses me of cruelty to animals, let me explain that I just used some **Dog Whisperer** tricks from the **National Geographic** channel to let the dog know who was the boss, and from then on the dog licked me instead of trying to tear my face off. If the dog is a Doberman or Pit Bull, seek professional advice, but be kind to your lady's pets.
- Never, ever, criticize your lady in public or make fun of her.
- Upon entering a restaurant, theatre, or public place try to locate the restroom immediately and not have your lady go searching for it later.
- Always carry mints, breath strips, etc., but do not offer one to your lady. (She might think that you think she needs one.) Rather be very obvious in taking one yourself and allow her to request one. Be careful what you eat before a date. Breaking wind is not romantic.
- Try kissing the back of your lady's hand. I know this seems old fashion, but many women report that they love this courtly gesture.
- Offer alcoholic beverages but never insist on her indulging. She might take you up on the offer just to try and drink you handsome. Most ladies want to be in complete control on first dates, and indeed, most dates.
- Never, ever drink too much alcohol in the presence of your date. One, it can be dangerous and illegal if you are driving,

and two, you could embarrass yourself (and especially her) in the presence of her friends or total strangers.

- Always immediately introduce your lady to your friends or associates in a public place. Never wait! Do it right away. Do not introduce a lady as your girlfriend unless there is no doubt that she is. Stick with "friend" at first. If she is your girlfriend, everyone will soon know by the way that she looks at you. Failure to make the introduction might signal to her that she is an embarrassment to you or unimportant.

- Never ask a lady her age, unless you are possibly dealing with a minor (otherwise known as "jail bait").

- When in conversation with your lady, always look her in the eye. Do not look away. Looking away shows disinterest, disrespect, and insincerity.

- When meeting your lady or picking her up for a date, always compliment her on her clothing and looks in general, even if you don't like the outfit.

- Flatter your lady, but do not be insincere. She will know if you are.

- When entering a restaurant or public place, lead your lady with a hand on the small of her back, but allow her to proceed ahead of you.

- When choosing seats in a restaurant, direct her to a seat, but reserve for yourself the seat which allows you to signal the wait staff. It could save you a stiff neck.

- Never park in a spot which has water on her side. Those shoes she is wearing likely cost a lot more than yours. This also applies to dirt or grass. Lead your lady around them. Heels frequently get stuck in mud or grass and can cause a lady to trip.

- Always offer your arm to your lady when walking together and especially at stairs. Position yourself to the middle, allowing her to take your arm and also reach the rail. Try walking downstairs in heels sometime and you will know why.

- Try and carry a spare coat/jacket/sweater in your car that she can use in times of cold weather or when the weather might suddenly change. She might not have checked the weather forecast, although you should always do so prior to a date.
- Carry an umbrella in your car.
- In the event of rain or other inclement weather always drive her to the door of your destination, get out, escort her to the lobby, then go and park your car. The reverse applies when leaving. Wet weather, even with an umbrella, can damage a coiffure (hairdo to southern gentlemen). You might also consider using valet parking when it is available.
- Never stare at sensitive parts of a woman's anatomy, even if she is displaying them proudly. An appreciative glance is sufficient.
- If your lady knocks over a glass or spills something in a public venue... take the blame on yourself. Men are expected to be clumsy.
- Never, ever, leave your lady unescorted in a public venue like a party with your friends. Stay by her side at all times.
- Never, ever, be late for picking up your lady, but also do not be early. She is likely getting ready right up until the last moment.
- When meeting your lady in a public place (i.e. restaurant, bar, etc.) always be early so that she will not have to be unescorted for a single second.
- When going to a new place, find out exactly where it is and how to get there. Running around looking for a place can be very uncomfortable to a lady. The neighborhood might be undesirable, or she may believe you have bad intentions. And if all else fails, try not to be a typical man....stop and ask for directions. **Why does it take 100 million sperm to fertilize an egg?** Because none will stop and ask for directions.

- Never assume you will get a kiss on the first date, but not offering one will sometimes offend a lady. Make a gentle move and allow her to accept or reject, and if a rejection is forthcoming then accept it gracefully.
- Always be willing to meet a lady's friends or family when she requests it of you. Her request for this is a sure sign that the relationship is progressing.
- Do not look or stare at other beautiful women in a public place, even if your lady is not present. Very bad form for a man to do so.
- At all times show your lady RESPECT. Show respect for her looks, her mind, her personality, her feelings, etc.
- Do not always, or even most of the time, ask a lady where she would like to go. Most ladies want to be led at first. If she is a true considerate lady, she will be reluctant to choose a place which might not be appropriate for your tastes or pocketbook. She also wants to find out your tastes and preferences as soon as possible. As the relationship progresses she will indicate her preferences.
- If you ask a lady out to a particular place or venue and she expresses reluctance, then be willing to suggest some alternatives. She may not wish to go to the symphony merely because she does not have the proper dress, or it is currently too tight or at the dry cleaners.
- In keeping with the above, always try to give a lady sufficient notice of a date which may require her to dress up. For a night at the opera, she may feel the need for a trip to her hairdresser, etc.
- Find out what your lady's interests are; ask questions, and get her talking about them. Then go and brush up on her interests. (Everything is on the Internet).
- Do not talk about ex girlfriends or ex wives, even if she talks about hers. Allow her to ask and then do not be critical of former women in your life.

- Do not assume that a "so so" first date ends the relationship. Remember that she is likely to be just as nervous as you are or perhaps more so. Do, however, try to put her at ease at all times.
- DO NOT LIE. Women are much better truth detectors than us males. Lies will also eventually catch up with you in an ongoing relationship. **What does a man consider honesty in a relationship?** Giving the woman his real name!
- Acceptable forms of prevarication (white lies which are really just charity) are compliments about her new hairdo, dress, weight loss, age (better guess younger or you are in big trouble), intelligence, etc.
- Men, do not think you are intellectually superior to ladies or try to show them that you are. Ladies frequently "act" much dumber than they are in an effort to keep our manly and very fragile egos intact.
- Ladies need a considerable amount or reassurance when it comes to a relationship. If you are in love with her, the recommended number of times you should tell her is seven times per day. If not in love but still in a serious relationship then you should call her at least once or twice per day just to let her know you are thinking of her. You should also compliment her, show affection, whisper sweet nothings on a regular basis, even if love is not as yet a part of the equation. An insecure lady is not much fun.
- A man should never tell a woman that he loves her if he does not. Throughout the ages, men have been telling this lie in order to advance their chances for sexual favors. It is not only dishonest, but downright mean. In matters of sex, most men are only seeking self gratification, but a woman is giving of herself in a very personal and intimate way. Telling a woman that you love her just for sex is wrong and more low than cheating at cards. Remember, in the old west they shot and hanged card cheats, and telling this lie is worse.

- At all times display Christian values towards your lady. Be sure to be kind, charitable, faithful, loving, honest, and generous. If you are not a Christian, use the principles anyway. Many other religions also contain similar principles of conduct toward women.

- Always greet your lady warmly. Smile and be sure to show her how happy you are to see her. A warm and affectionate greeting can set the tone for a date or a whole day.

- DANCE with your lady. Most women love to dance. If you don't dance, then learn. If you do not have a chance to learn then have her teach you or at the very least hold her tight on the dance floor and shuffle your feet, but TAKE HER OUT ON THE DANCE FLOOR.

- Always say complimentary things about your lady to others and never discuss sexual matters with anyone else. Most men who brag about their sexual prowess are lying. The man who actually has a good sex life just smiles quietly to himself.

- Keep shows of public affection to a minimum. Many ladies are uncomfortable with this. Allow her to take the lead in this. She will show you her level of comfort in this matter, but should she display public affection then you damn well better return it in kind. Some ladies I interviewed have disagreed with a man not immediately showing public affection. Use your best judgment guys.

- Always dress as well as you can for the occasion. A woman may want to show you off to friends as much as you do. A well dressed and well groomed man shows a woman that he cares and takes time to look good for her. I hope you men realize that the amount of time we may take preparing for a date is miniscule compared to the effort most ladies take.

- Be a good listener. Sometimes a lady will want to vent anger, but not on the subject she is actually upset about. Go with it and do not always assume that it is a problem that can be solved (Which is what men typically want to do). Just allow her to vent and you listen.

- The previous can be especially true when your lady returns from her hair dresser. Many women are unhappy. Be kind, tell her it looks fine and just allow her to heap scorn on that female dog who did not follow her instructions and destroyed her self esteem. Within a few days she may actually be happy with the look.

- Ask for your lady's advice on anything; business, dress, a problem, etc. The idea is to show her that you value her opinion and she is a necessary part of your life. A woman has a sense that she is there to complete you and believe me a good woman does exactly that.

- In keeping with the above, if you receive awards or recognition in your life from others, make sure that you publicly and privately acknowledge the lady in your life. Regardless of the recognition, she was a part of your success whether you know it or not.

- I may be stating the obvious, but always show sincere appreciation for anything that your lady does for you. If it is a home cooked meal then thank her at the very least. If it is tasty tell her how much you enjoyed it. If it almost made you gag, try not to gag and learn to cook meals for the two of you. If the meal poisoned you, I hope you survived, and if not, you are not reading this book anyway. Always thank her for anything she does for you, from doing your laundry, to not bothering you during that football game on TV.

- Always encourage your lady on anything she undertakes to do. Never be negative or say the words "I don't believe you can do that". You expect encouragement from her on your job and other tasks, so give it to her.

- Be a friend to your lady. Treat her like your other close friends. It has been said that a bra is like a good friend. It is next to your heart and provides good support.

- When meeting a lady at a venue, especially at night, find out when she is arriving via cell phone and meet her in the parking lot and escort her in. Then always escort her to her vehicle and stay until she pulls away. Cars sometimes do not start and you need to be there in case it does not.
- Never compete with a woman on any level. You are looking for a partner not a competitor. If you are smarter than her she will recognize and appreciate the fact without you using every six syllable word in the dictionary. Then again, be advised that many ladies make an effort to make us feel more intelligent than we are (They dummy down just a bit) just so our fragile male egos will not suffer bruising. The competition clause also applies to games and sports. As a man you may hit the golf ball further or strike a tennis ball with more pace, but do not be competitive with your lady in this situation. Compliment her frequently when she does well, slow yourself down a bit, and don't bother to keep score unless she insists. The best thing to do is find a game or sport in which to participate in which she is equally good or better than you.
- If your relationship has progressed to a point where you ask for her opinion on where to go to eat, always have an opinion of your own and be ready to express it if she says she has no preference. Women dislike indecision in a man. If you truly don't care and wish to find out her preferences, then make three suggestions from which she can choose. If she still has no preference, then make the call. A true lady wants you to choose. She wants this for two reasons; first so that you are making the financial choice based on what you have in your wallet, and secondly to discover your preference for the type of place which may be loud, fun or romantic. You are asking her out, not the other way around.
- Do not take a lady to loud restaurants or bars on the first few dates. You need a quiet place in which to get to know each other with verbal communication. Always remember

that talk is not cheap to a woman; she wants it. Talk is also not cheap when you hire a divorce lawyer.

- Do not try to instruct a woman in anything unless she specifically requests your help. You may be a low handicap golfer, but do not try to teach her unless she asks for it. On the other hand, most ladies will welcome an opportunity to instruct you in something at which they are good, so find out what she is good at and ask her about it.
- Do not deny a lady a trip to the restroom or cause her to wait, if you can possibly avoid it. All men should realize that much more can occur in there than just nature.
- Be humorous with your lady. It is very high on most women's lists as a trait which they desire in men. This does not mean tell her bawdy jokes. If you are not naturally a witty or fun guy, then learn to be. Find some good clean jokes and learn how to tell them well.
- Always try to anticipate a lady's needs. This may be as simple as stopping at a gas station on a long trip together when you don't need gas or having bottled water in a cooler on this trip. Being able to provide for a lady before she makes the request will go a long way.
- Keep a supply of facial tissue at your dwelling and in your car. Women have all kinds of uses for this. Toilet paper and paper towels are just not as good.
- Don't be afraid to carry a woman's purse when she needs for you to do so. She is the one you are trying to impress. Others don't matter.
- Following a meal, if a woman has spinach between her teeth, tell her in a gentle manner and instruct her to do likewise for you. If she has it in her teeth, you might also try asking her to look at your teeth. She will likely take the hint and you could save her some embarrassment.
- Exhibit proper table manners at all times. If you don't know what they are, then learn.
- Never call your woman "my old lady". PERIOD!

- Never stop trying to learn about your lady, even if you are married for 75 years. The more you learn the better relationship you will have. We men are rather simple creatures, but I can assure you that the depths of a woman's heart, soul, and mind remain for most of us largely unexplored territory.

- Don't freak out if your lady cries and you don't know why. Sometimes she just may need a good cry for a variety of reasons or no reason at all. Comfort her, hold her and let her tell you what it is about if she is willing to do so, but be willing to just accept it with no explanation. Just tell her that you understand, even if you do not. **What's the difference between men and mascara?** No difference…they both run at the first sign of emotion!

- Ask for and take some photographs of your lady. Always ask for a wallet or framed photo of a lady you are serious about. If she does not produce one then take some pictures of her. Many ladies enjoy posing for photographs, and it allows you to document your relationship, have keepsakes and remember good times when you need to.

- Never forget to hug and cuddle with your lady on a frequent basis. I do not know why this is so important to most females, but it appears to be in most cases, so just do it.

- On the first date note the color of the lady's eyes, compliment her on them and continue to do so throughout your relationship. Eyes are very important to a woman. Most ladies tend to want to look in the eyes of someone who is speaking to them. If you don't believe this try following a car load of women where the driver is engaged in the conversation. Exercise extreme caution.

- If you sense a potential conflict or argument arising with your lady, always seek to try and turn it to humor, if possible. You can quickly diffuse a potential bomb, which if exploded can cause you serious harm.

- Never, ever show anger toward another woman in the presence of your lady. Even if the waitress spills the marinara sauce all over the front of your best suit try not to react in anger. Your lady could take this as a sign that you are potentially abusive with women.

- If you ever have your lady over to your place for a dinner or rental movie evening, have the lights dimmed down or use some candles. Have you ever wondered why most night clubs and good restaurants have low lighting levels? Past the age of 21, most ladies begin to be concerned about their facial looks and the possibility of small lines in their face. Low light softens their appearance and erases many lines. It is important for a lady to feel like she looks attractive to you, and she will generally be more comfortable in a low light environment. You want her to be comfortable. (Who knows...you may look better in low light too, although I wouldn't count on it.) Do not, however, make the lighting so low as to appear seductive.

- If married, you will also want to keep the lights low in the bedroom. Statistics show that the vast majority of women are unhappy with their bodies. Granted us males are visually oriented when it comes to sex, but ask yourself what is more important; a dazzling view of your lady's body which may excite you, but makes your lady self conscious, or a lady who is very comfortable in bed under soft lighting? Who do think will be more fun? If, however, your lady is very happy with her body, then by all means bring on the flood lights.

- Share your toys with your lady. Always be open to her wanting to get interested in your activities. The difference between men and boys is the price of their toys. She probably won't break any, but be on alert.

- Be a mature man in your thinking and actions with your lady. **It has been said that the difference between a man and a U.S. Savings Bond, is that the bond eventually matures.**

General Do's, Don'ts and Observations...

The following is a listing of general ideas on what resides in the mind of a woman. I do not pretend to have any special knowledge in the area. In fact, I believe that any man who claims to have even a working knowledge of the feminine mind is either delusional or a blatant liar. Remember always, however, that our masculine inability to understand women is part of their charm and attractive nature. To paraphrase **Forrest Gump**; Ladies "are like a box of chocolates, you never know what you are going to get". Guys... relish and enjoy the mystery of the female psyche.

True Romance is in the Details

While I was interviewing ladies for this book, the most common response I heard about what women considered romantic was attention to details. The devil is not in the details, but true romance may be. For most ladies, the small things make the difference, not large extravagant gifts or expensive vacations. Doing small things to show her that you are thinking about or care about her every day is romantic. Show her that you are thoughtful. Merely arising early some morning to have her coffee ready when she awakens can set the tone for a whole day.

Comfort Levels

Always remember that you are the man in the relationship, and with all due deference to the lady who is a black belt in martial arts or a serious iron pumper, you are most likely larger and stronger than her. As such, when a woman accepts a date with a man, she is potentially risking much. In her mind there exists the possibility of you being a serial rapist, an abuser, or worse. Do all that you can to reassure her at all times that your intentions are honorable. Put her at ease.

If in your relationship you are having dates at each other's residence, always remember that the lady will typically feel more comfortable at her place as opposed to yours.

Be a gentleman. You can be exciting and still be a gentleman in every sense of the word.

Things to Know About Women in General

A woman is different from you in her psychological makeup and her view of a relationship with a man. When she appears to be upset and you ask her what is wrong, the most common reply is a sharp "Nothing!", especially if she is upset with you. She believes that you should already know what you have done wrong, and unfortunately, most of us men do not have a clue. Be patient and allow her to explain. Always listen carefully to your lady and try to read between the lines. Fully evaluate what she has been saying recently and look for subtle clues as to what may have caused her to be upset.

The Apology.   Guys…Suck it up and Grovel

When in the course of human events you do something really stupid to irritate and make your lady mad, and you will (It is not a matter of if, only when), then swallow the manly pride, apologize sincerely and grovel. I have asked numerous ladies what they want from a man when he screws up. The two most common responses were diamonds and groveling. Few of us can afford the diamonds and this was said by several ladies in jest, but also says something about the cynical nature many have today.

By groveling I do not mean cease being a man, but put forth an effort into the apology. Say it many times and try to assure her that what you did will not happen again. Indicate that you know how it hurt her and understand her feelings. Take her venom, which she may still have, calmly and do not fire back or try to make excuses for your behavior. If you truly wish to diffuse the bomb wrapped up in your lady, show contrition, continue to apologize, tell her that she is right to be mad, and above all speak calmly. Do this and her anger will quickly recede. If you do not, then you will just as quickly see that "Hell hath no fury like a woman scorned."

Apologize Anyway (Even when you are not wrong)

Okay, so your lady is mad at you and you have done nothing wrong. This can happen. Sometimes your lady, due to other stresses or physical factors can just experience depression or may be mad at something which she considers to be somewhat silly. She is not truly mad at you, but you may be the closest target, and she redirects her anger at you. Try and recognize these times and start by saying that you understand her feelings and apologize. By all means this does not mean you should admit to doing something wrong which you have not done. Apologize to her for the sun not shining that day, for the bad breath you had last week, or just don't be specific at all, but apologize. You can sometimes quickly diffuse a bomb that you do not want going off.

A joke has circulated on the Internet which says, the difference between a terrorist and a woman with PMS is that you can negotiate with a _____. Fill in the blank for yourself.

Needs and Burdens

Find a need in your lady's life and fulfill that need. Find a burden in her life and lift it from her, even if it is for one day. Seek these out. A need might be something as simple as a wall hook in the laundry room or it might be a very sincere hug. You can never ever hug your lady too much. A need might also be that timely romantic vacation or a night out with her lady friends while you watch the kids.

Burdens can be the daily chores she has or a problem at her place of employment. A burden could also be when she wrecked the car and you have not fully forgiven her for it. Try to relieve her of some burden each day.

For both needs and burdens find out what they are for your lady. If they are not apparent then ask her. She may not tell you right away, but probe gently, listen and you will soon find out.

The Crisis

Be calm and loving in the face of a crisis. Many of us men react badly. Allow me to describe what I once did. My wife called me at work to tell me that she had just had an automobile accident which was her fault. My first reactions were anger and concern for the car. I totally neglected to ask about her well being or if she was hurt in any way. Most of us have experienced a car accident and even if you are not hurt physically, you are very much shaken.

A certain woman told me that she locked her keys in the car and had to call her husband out of work on a very busy day. She expected a tirade from him, but instead received understanding and his immediate departure from work to assist her. She told me that she has never loved him so much as that day and has remembered it always.

Be the Hero for Your Lady

The man above was a hero to his lady and rescued her. Most of the great blockbuster movies of our time involve a man who is a hero and rescues his lady. It may not mean that you save her from drowning or anything this dramatic, but you can still be the hero on almost a daily basis. Changing the oil in her car can sometimes make you her hero. Be the hero for your lady!

Conversation

Women crave this from their men. It is important to most ladies and a topic about which they frequently complain. Be a good listener, but also let your lady know what is going on with you. When your lady is quiet, your likely first concern is that she may be mad at you. Make sure you understand she may feel the same way when you are quiet. The strong silent type is good for Hollywood, but only practice being strong with your lady.

The Toilet Seat Controversy

This book is only about what we men should do for the ladies in our lives. Undoubtedly women should also do some things for us, but I do not address these issues. I will, however, side with men about this all important and ongoing controversy concerning the toilet seat being up or down. I do not care if it is dark or not, I will always check to see if a toilet seat is down before I attempt to seat myself. Likewise, I will always make sure it is up if I am using the toilet, but not sitting. Even you ladies will check to see if the lid is down. Sorry ladies, but I do not see this as sole male responsibility. String me up if you like. I am on the guy side of this issue.

What Women Want

Can anyone answer this question for me? It has been scientifically shown that due to varying hormone levels in a woman, their tastes in men will change over the course of a month; at times wanting a very masculine man and at other times, a softer man. This comes from the **Discovery** channel which cites other studies.

In the movie **Bedazzled,** starring Brendan Fraser and Elizabeth Hurley, Ms. Hurley plays the devil who offers wishes to Mr. Fraser in return for his soul as he pursues a female co-worker. This is a very funny movie which offers some insights into women along with the comedy. At one point Fraser's character, Elliot remarks that he does not think that women know what they want. To which Ms. Hurley, as Satan, replies "Amen".

The movie comedy **What Women Want,** starring Mel Gibson, also explores this question, but does not offer any conclusions. I believe that on many levels, it is true that what a woman wants can change from day to day or even from hour to hour. My only advice to men is that you be on your toes, understand this about women, and go with the flow. A woman's prerogative is to change her mind. Just try placing furniture for her.

One thing I am certain that women do want is to be desired. And I don't just mean in a sexual manner. Show her that you desire her mind, her soul, her intellect, and her personality as well as her body. Just think how you as a man feels when your lady expresses desire for you.

It is hoped that the following pages describe some of what women do want from the man in their life. Try it and you might like the results you get.

Big
Romantic
Ideas

Flowers...

Typically most women love flowers. They love the beauty, the color, and the fragrance. Numerous scientific studies have shown that the female nose is more sensitive than that of the male. But most importantly is that women love the thoughtfulness behind the effort which shows that the man is thinking of her, and this is why it is so important to give flowers on days other than special occasions when flowers might normally be expected.

A flower for every date!

When first dating a lady consider the idea of bringing her a single flower for each date. It can be an inexpensive carnation, a flower picked up by the roadside, or a rose. It does not have to be wrapped or in a vase. The lady will likely have a container for it. A flower picked from your garden is also quite nice. Consider planting a rose bush for this purpose.

Roses for the first year!

Mark the day of your first date and bring her one rose for the first month's anniversary, then two roses for the second month, etc. At the end of the year she will have earned a full dozen. Then continue this tradition as the relationship grows on an annual basis, with 13 roses for the second year, 14 for the third, etc. You might try having one additional rose in a different color as a promise for the years to come.

Flowers for no special reason!

Always endeavor to bring her flowers on days that do not represent special occasions (i.e. Valentine's Day, Anniversary, etc.) While it is very appropriate to do so on these days, try doing it on a day when she needs a lift (i.e. hard day at work for her, an unhappy day, etc.)

Flowers delivered to her place of employment!

If your lady works, then on one of the non-occasion days have flowers delivered to her at work. Do not bring them yourself, but rather spend the extra money to have them specially delivered. She will have the envy of every one of her female co-workers, and you will get respect from the same.

Flowers to say that you are sorry!

Depending on the nature of the offense you may have them flung in your face, so break the thorns off of the roses, but consider this when making a sincere effort to apologize. Even if they are rejected, give it a try, but also never let flowers be the whole apology. Say the words, too!

Remember that "every kiss" does not have to begin with jewelry. Flowers thoughtfully given can work just as well. Even though flowers are transitory and will soon wilt, this is part of their appeal. Always remember that a woman is like a flower. Nurture her and she will come to full bloom, do not and she will also wilt.

A Special Note!

Try this idea. Give her a dozen roses and include in the middle a cloth reproduction of a rose chosen for its authenticity. The note should say something to the effect of "My love for you will endure until all of the roses are gone."

Now a Word of Caution...Don't Overdo It!

While I am a big advocate of giving your lady flowers on a frequent basis, I must now caution you that flowers given too frequently will soon lose their appeal, and become routine. It is therefore advised that you vary your gifts, vary the type of flowers given or sometimes take a break from giving them at all.

Make Her a Romantic Dinner...

What makes a man think about a candlelight dinner? A power failure!

The operable word here is "make". Make her a dinner with your own hands. Now it is understood that many of the male species have limited cooking skills, but it is my contention that every man can make something, or at least he can get instructions on how to prepare a nice dish from his mother or a female friend. As a last resort read a cook book, go on line or learn how to make something. No excuses guys!

The lady in question will most likely appreciate the effort even if the food is less than palatable.

Do not try out a new dish on your lady without having cooked it successfully at least once before.

DO'S AND DON'TS OF A HOMEMADE DINNER...

- Do spare no expense; get good quality ingredients and good wines, etc.
- Do set the table as best as your equipment and budget will allow. Cloth napkins, extra forks, candles, flowers, best silverware, glassware, and plates, etc.
- Do lower the lights, but not to the point that she can't find the plate
- Do have some scented candles burning elsewhere, not too close to the table, but also have table candles (unscented on the table for that romantic feel). Do not place the candles

or flowers directly between you. You will just end up having to move them.

- Do plate the food and do not serve out of serving dishes (i.e. make it like a good restaurant experience)
- Do serve ice water in separate glasses from the other drinks
- Do end the meal with a good dessert (Store bought okay here)
- Do provide rolls or side bread (She may need it to push with)
- Be attentive to her drink levels and keep her glasses refilled
- Do seat her properly and unseat her
- Do try to find out her likes and dislikes (This home cooked meal should not be offered until well into the relationship and you know she will be comfortable being at your bachelor pad.)
- The above statement presupposes a dating relationship and not marriage, but for you married men keep the sparks flying and make a good meal like this for your wife on a frequent basis.
- Do have soft music playing, and it highly recommended that you dance with her between courses or at the end of the meal. Even if you do not dance, just cuddle her and rock back and forth to the music.

DON'TS

- Do not serve a meal that will require her to eat with her fingers
- Do not serve any food which might create pressure in the gastrointestinal tract (no beans or anything like them guys)
- Do not serve highly spiced food unless she has shown a significant love for it.

- Try not to serve raw onions or large amounts of garlic in the food.
- Place mints on the table, but also have a clean new toothbrush prominently displayed in the guest bathroom along with a new tube of tooth paste and briefly mention it to her if the food was highly spiced. Don't make a big deal of this, but just mention it at the end of the meal, but never after having just kissed your lady.
- Do not insist on constantly refilling her wine glass if she indicates she has had enough. She may misinterpret your intentions.
- Do not let her help with any cleanup or clearing of the table even if she insists upon it. Be a man and thank her for the offer, but do not let her near the dishes. Pile them up in the sink and continue the romance.
- Do not be offended if she does not clean her plate. Your cooking may be lousy, but most likely she is trying not to act like a pig in front of you. Then again, if she keels over gagging after the first bite you may want your next meal to be catered.

Cook a meal at her house!

If by chance you fancy yourself to be a good cook then offer to cook a meal at her house or have her over early to watch you cook at yours. More than one woman has stated that she considers watching a man cooking to be sexy and highly romantic. Allow her to watch and even make suggestions, but do not allow her to help. That expensive frock she is wearing could get stained.

Also if you have an apron, put it on during this cooking to keep you from spilling something on yourself.

Shopping...

I sincerely hope no ladies take offense at the assumption that women do frequently enjoy the art of shopping. Men are the hunters and women are the gatherers. Guys please understand that in general ladies like this activity even if they do not purchase anything at all. So use this to your advantage to provide an enjoyable day or evening for your lady.

Take her shopping if you are in need of clothes!

Especially if you are in need of clothes. Solicit her advice on your selections, although she will likely offer them whether solicited or not. She will also likely have a flare for fashion and a better idea of what looks good on you than you do. Remember that some women played with Barbie and Ken dolls when they were young, so allow her to accessorize you. In the movie **Steel Magnolias**, the character played by Shirley MacLaine stated that the only difference between us and the lower life forms is our ability to accessorize.

What do you immediately know about a well dressed man?
His wife or girlfriend selected his clothes!

If at a mall, be sure to stop by men's cologne and let her test out some samples on you, so don't put any cologne on before you make this trip.

Take her shopping anyway!

Even if you don't have a need for anything for you, still take her to a mall to shop. It is good exercise, she will likely enjoy the experience even if nothing is purchased, you will get some good ideas for future gifts for her, and you will be able to discern her preferences and your degree of future financial commitment if she proves to have very expensive tastes.

Make sure to visit some clothing stores for her and also some jewelry and perfume stores. Depending on the length of your relationship it might be fun to visit Victoria's Secret, but be prepared to leave immediately if your lady shows any discomfort. I once purchased some under garments for my wife before Christmas and the 18 year old sales girl asked if I wanted them wrapped, to which I replied "No thank you, I'll just eat them here!" I had to start laughing and show her I was joking just before she pushed the security alarm. I could have been arrested, but the shocked look on her face was indeed priceless.

Take her grocery shopping!

Plan a meal that you can both cook together and take her shopping at a grocery store. You can also learn about her this way. You can learn her tastes in food, her bargain hunting abilities, and you will also likely pick up some useful hints about cooking for yourself.

If the wallet permits, take her to specialty food stores or the increasing number of stores that cater to high end tastes and try preparing a meal together.

Take her to a Flea Market!

This is always a good idea on how to spend a day with your lady.

Take her to some antique malls or shops!

Or at least some shops where they have old stuff. You can learn a lot about your lady based on her reactions to things that she sees.

You may discover how romantic she is. Even if she is not especially into antiques, most ladies will find this to be an enjoyable experience. Guys remember to be patient and always show admiration for the things she notices.

Take her to buy a dress!

This suggestion will be largely dependent upon your wallet and the type of dress which may or may not be needed for a special date or occasion. Let's assume that you have asked her out to a special dance or a nice restaurant. Even if she has an extensive wardrobe, suggest taking her to one or more shops for a new dress. Suggest a price range if she asks. She will then know where to go. Then have her try on multiple dresses even if you like the first one she selects. She will enjoy the experience of trying them on for you, and you get to have some input into her selection. After all you are paying for it.

Notes:

- Do not ever accompany your lady to buy a swimsuit or suggest buying one for her. Even if your lady has a figure better than a fashion model she is unlikely to think so, and buying a swimsuit for most ladies is a traumatic experience.
- Most guys think their body is great although as one comedian put it "In a man's bikini type swimsuit most of us look like a Bartlett pear with a rubber band around it".

The Unexpected Trip...

This romantic interlude requires a great deal of planning and investigation, but I assure you it can have a significant impact on your lady. First, it should not be attempted until you have a strong committed relationship or you are married. Secondly, you need to know quite a lot about your lady's likes and dislikes. Finally you may need a deep pocketbook, although lesser cost alternatives to the example depicted below can be employed.

Allow me to describe a scenario and list some dos and don'ts.

You have totally cleared this with her boss at her place of employment so she is allowed some time off. You say you are taking her to lunch on a Friday and pick her up. Instead of lunch you take her to the airport. If married, make sure you have packed for her clothes, makeup, etc. Get another woman (preferably a relative) to help. If not married then get a girlfriend of hers or a relative, but be prepared to spend some money once you reach your destination on the items you have failed to bring.

The two of you get on a plane for a romantic destination and spend an enjoyable weekend together which was totally unexpected by her.

As stated this requires effort and significant planning, but if you can make the proper arrangements and anticipate most of her needs, she will remember the event forever and truly appreciate the effort you have made.

DO'S

- Do make sure that her calendar is clear for the weekend and have all matters taken care of. (i.e. boarding of pets, babysitter for kids, etc.)
- Do make all efforts to have what she will need for the weekend in terms of clothing, makeup, other sundries, etc.
- Do let her boss or close associates at work know what you are doing. Enlist the help of a close female friend at work who will subsequently sing your praises to all other workers.
- Do have all reservations covered.
- Do have an alternate later flight in mind in case the unexpected arises which will create a need for a return trip to her house.
- If not married have a reservation for an additional hotel room and let her know it right away. (This, of course, depends on the type of relationship you have)
- Do get her back at a reasonable time on Sunday.
- Do stress that she contact a close friend or relative about the event. You do not want to be accused of kidnapping should an unexpected need arise.

DON'TS

- Don't immediately tell her where you are going. She will likely figure that out at the airport.
- Don't insist and be prepared to cancel if something unanticipated arises and then be gracious.
- Don't allow her to worry about any responsibility she has back home. Take care of everything.

This type of event can work at almost any income level. The trip could be by automobile to a nearby town or even to a local hotel. The point of this exercise is the unexpected nature of it. You have seen your lady or others on Christmas morning opening a wrapped gift. Take a look at her face and imagine being able to see that look for a whole weekend.

Gifts...

Gifts, other than flowers, are important to a lady. They are most often something tangible that she can remember for the rest of her life and a reflection of your feelings toward her. Be very careful in what you buy your lady and how often you do so. Special occasions are not the only time a gift should be given and when you do buy, be thoughtful and put forth an effort in your selection.

Candy!

Scientific studies indicate that women have a somewhat similar reaction to chocolate as they do in love and sex. But for most it is a true "love/hate" relationship. In this day and time ladies are constantly under pressure to look younger and thinner. As a result most women are forever dieting and a gift of candy is more temptation than most would like to have.

Therefore should you make a gift of candy to your lady (Who is not thin and trim or upon standing sideways and sticking out her tongue looks like a zipper) I would suggest the following. Either buy small quantities of premium chocolate or a larger quantity given at her place of employment or just before she has an event with other women. This gives her a chance to sample what she likes without too much guilt and yet share with her friends or colleagues. You will also get respect from her peers and impress them.

Greeting Cards!

Give them often! They are inexpensive, cover all occasions or none, and are tangible. Of course give them when the occasion demands (i.e. Valentine's Day, Anniversary, etc.), but give them when they are unexpected. A card sent in the mail to a lady at her work place which just expresses a sentiment of you thinking about her can be more appreciated than you imagine. Pick them out with care at the store and always include a personal note.

Avoid most humorous cards. They may be wildly funny to you, but will never express romantic sentiments to your lady. Also do not give cards about age, a very sensitive subject with most ladies.

Personal Gifts!

Make your gifts personal and show an effort in the time you spent selecting it. We are not talking about gifts from **Victoria's Secret,** which may or may not be appropriate for your relationship status. Depending on your financial condition your gifts may vary, but always choose quality. It is better to give a smaller item of high quality than a large gift of poor quality. Ladies notice this. I once paid $1,000 more for a string of pearls by "Mikimoto" as compared to a lesser known label, which to my untrained eye, appeared to have equal quality. Why would I do this? After investigating pearls extensively (Didn't have a clue at first), I came to the conclusion that my lady would often be wearing the pearls at rather formal occasions with her hair up, and other women would notice the little "Mikimoto" tag at the back of her neck. I wouldn't care, but I know she did. If nothing else it told other women that I was a man who cared about my lady and appreciated quality and label.

If retailers put a Michael Jordan label on a pair of ordinary jeans for men, few of us would give a damn, and certainly would not pay twice as much for this label. Women, however, sometimes will and do pay extra for a label even if the quality is not there.

Try to find unique gifts which match your lady's taste. Some very nice gifts can be had for lesser money if you take the time to find them. Carefully consider what you have seen about your lady (i.e. her preferences in jewelry, accessories, colognes, etc.

Notes:

- Always wrap your gift for a lady even if you are a lousy wrapper. Do not place the gift in a bag with tissue on top. Wrapping will always increase the pleasure of receiving the gift.
- Don't be too extravagant with your giving. It may make your lady feel uncomfortable if she is unable to respond in kind. Indeed, it makes her feel obligated to repay in other ways. I remind you again that this book is not about doing things for a lady so that sex will be your reward. Not all kisses or all sex begins with "Kay".

Jewelry

Jewelry is almost always a gift which is appreciated by a lady. Jewelry is a big part of the accessories and most women will tell you that accessories make the outfit. Before buying jewelry, however, check your bank account and be prepared for sticker shock. Do not waste your time with costume jewelry or pieces of low quality and workmanship.

If at all possible seek another woman's help (one of approximately the same age who knows your lady), try to be aware of what type of jewelry your lady already wears (her tastes), and visit multiple stores to compare values. This is usually a substantial purchase so shop carefully. If the object of your affection is well to do and has an extensive collection of large diamonds, do not attempt to purchase ¼ carat diamond stud ear rings for her. She may appreciate the effort, but will likely never wear them except in your presence. If your check book does not allow you to purchase jewelry of equal quality to what she wears, then consider other gifts.

If, however, you are considering marriage and will be buying an engagement ring, consult with numerous jewelers. There is generally a formula for how much you can afford which is tied to your current salary. Know the formula and use it to determine what you will buy up to its limit. Don't go cheap. It is hoped that she will be wearing it for the rest of her life.

Always remember the song "Diamonds are a girl's best friend".

The Kind of Gifts which are not Wrapped

Not all gifts to your lady need to be tangible or something that she can touch. Consider some of the gifts which are detailed herein. Give her a day off from chores and do them yourself, wash the dishes when she does not expect it, or give her a night out with her girlfriends and you watch the kids. These are wonderful gifts to give to your lady and require no money, just your effort.

The Massage or Spa Treatment and Similar Stuff...

Giving your lady a massage can be a gift of relaxation, pure physical pleasure, a healing of tired muscles, or a very sensual experience often leading to additional pleasures for the both of you. The nature of your relationship should define the type of massage that is appropriate and not an experience which is seen as suggestive or seductive when it is inappropriate.

Giving any kind of massage as simply foreplay for sex can remove some of the pleasure for a woman if she perceives your ultimate goal to be seduction. Rather than relaxing and pleasuring her, she may be on edge. Sometimes a good body massage can be an effective and highly sensual prelude to sex, but no matter how long you have been in the relationship, a good massage given to your lady by you can be much appreciated.

Make it your goal to sometimes just give a massage to your lady and expect nothing in return except her well being and appreciation.

The Foot Massage or Piggy Pull

Men, try walking around in high heels or even low heels for ten minutes. High heels were not invented by women or for their comfort. They were originally designed to make a lady's rear end protrude more, but also offer the visual benefit for us men of more curvaceous legs. Most women also tend to spend more time on their feet doing the things which need to be done while their mate resides on the couch imitating a potato in front of the weekly NFL, NBA, MLB, NHL, or whatever offering. Your lady's feet will often be tired.

Have your lady remove her shoes, hose, socks, etc. from her feet and if she feels it necessary, have her wash them or you do it for her in a foot bath with the appropriate salts or foot soothing ingredients. After all Jesus washed the feet of his disciples.

Have her lie down with her feet in your lap or recline on a cushion from her chair. Apply the appropriate body oil or baby powder (My preference) to her feet with a towel underneath. Kneed her feet and toes and indeed pull and stretch her toes until you find the spots where she has the most pleasure. Having her close her eyes is a good thing, although if you do this right, she will close them without being prompted. Continue until she "begs" you to stop. A lady will frequently think you are getting tired before she is ready for you to quit and thus suggest that you do. Keep going until she really means it.

Working your way up the ladder, you may also, (depending on the status of your relationship) massage her lower legs. Going above her lower legs to her thighs should not be done until you are at the point of doing a full body massage. A woman's thighs are a private and sensuous part of her body and thought by most women to be too large even if they are not.

The Back and Neck Massage

Following a long and tiring day this is also a good thing to do for your lady. Remember, however, that she is a lady and do not apply the force or techniques used by the large hairy football trainer you had in high school.

I am not a massage therapist and have no licenses to do so. Therefore I can not advise as to the techniques to be employed. It does not, however, take a genius to gently massage your lady's neck or upper back and shoulders. It also does not require the removal of any of her clothing or an air of seduction. So just do it for her to ease her aches and pains and show her your affection.

The Full Massage or Treatment

As I stated before I am not an expert on massage therapy, but should your relationship be at a level where a full body massage can be given by you to your lady then read up on the techniques, learn how to do it right and do it without any expectation of sex as a follow up.

I would also suggest a setting similar to that as outlined in the Bubble Bath section. Low lights, candles, soft relaxing music, an appropriate beverage, and rose petals.

The Spa Treatment

Depending on your financial resources please consider the idea of sending your lady to a spa for a full day's treatment. There are a wide variety of packages which can be purchased by you as a gift for your lady. Half day, full day, manicure, pedicure, facial, massage, etc. Check out what you can afford, your lady's availability in time, and get a spa package for her. Make sure her schedule is clear or take it upon yourself to do the things which need to be done.

In fact, try and find a day when she will be attending to ordinary chores (i.e. grocery shopping, taking the kids to soccer practice, house cleaning, laundry, etc.) and then surprise her with the spa treatment and the knowledge that you will be doing all of these chores. The day will then indeed be very special for her. Imagine, she was facing a day of drudgery and you replaced a dreaded day with one of full and complete relaxation for her.

Shampoo Her Hair

Some evening after a long day, try giving your lady a shampoo. She does not necessarily need to be in the shower or tub, or even be disrobed for you to do this. She can wear a bathrobe and simply bend her over the sink to wet her hair. Hair stylists do this, by bending you backwards. It can be done forwards, then have her sit in a comfortable chair (A lawn chair works well) with towels underneath to catch any run off.

Use her special shampoo and any conditioner she likes. You are likely not an expert in this, but don't worry about it. Just reach deeply to her scalp and massage her head and keep piling up her hair on top. She will likely have to step into the shower afterwards to get all of the soap out and repair the tangled mess you made of her hair, but do not fret. It's the effort she will appreciate along with the sensual and relaxing pleasure you have given her.

Brush Her Hair

Women often spend a considerable amount of time brushing their hair to improve its quality, or they would if they had the time in this busy world in which we live. Try sitting her down one evening just prior to bed time or for that matter at any time and just brush her hair gently for about a half hour or so. Position her on the floor between your legs while you sit on a couch or chair and just brush or better yet, have her show you how she wants it done. I assure you that for most ladies you will soon having them purring like a well contented kitty cat.

Massage Her Head

Depending on the length and thickness of her hair try giving her a scalp massage. Do not do it if it will destroy a recent visit to her hair dresser or you will create major tangles.

Paint Her Toe Nails

Try to paint her toe nails for her. You will likely screw it up, but the effort will be appreciated and be very relaxing for her. Try to pretend to paint your own toe nails, and you will quickly realize the difficult nature of the task for her.

Scratch her Back

Even if she doesn't need it just try it occasionally. It can sooth the frazzled nerves.

The Bubble Bath...

This concept is, of course, suitable for committed relationships or in a marriage venue. It should not be employed as a potential lead up to sex as an end result. The bath is for her and a chance to totally relax. Do not even hint that it is a tool for seduction, which could place her on edge if she is not in the mood. This is her time and do not intrude once you have set it up.

Women today are hard working either inside the home, outside of it or most frequently both. Picture your lady having come home from a hard day at work or having dealt with children and all of the other issues that make for a hectic schedule. Give her this time to be alone and away from the daily cares of the world.

To make it a memorable experience get scented candles, a nice fruity wine or champagne (if she drinks), a single flower in a vase, rose petals, relaxing music and a nice scented bubble bath product or bath treatment.

Light the candles and place them on or around the tub at the faucet end (She will be lying in the tub facing the candles and can see them flicker). Scatter the rose petals around the edge of the tub and on the floor leading to the tub. Do not put the petals in the tub. Place the flower where she can see it.

Arrange the lighting in the room so that the candles are the predominant light, but do not make it so dark that she could hurt herself getting into the tub.

Place a rolled up towel at the point where her head will be for cushioning as she lays down in the tub. This can also help prevent her hair from getting wet as she relaxes. Also place a full size bath towel where she can easily reach it from the bath.

Place the wine (A nice cup of hot tea, or cold beverage she likes are also appropriate) in a convenient spot where she can reach it.

Turn on the relaxing music at a low volume level.

Surprise makes this effort all the more rewarding, so make every effort to not let her know what you have prepared.

Lead her to the bathroom door with her fully clothed, kiss her gently, tell her that you want her to relax and then leave, but let her know where you will be and that you will not be disturbing her.

She will return when she is ready, but may also fall asleep for a while. This is what you want for her.

Notes:

- Make the bath water hotter than you think it should be. It will cool quickly anyway, but caution her about the heat. She can always add cool water quickly if it is too hot.
- Rose petals can now be purchased in most grocery stores that have a floral department. No need to buy a rose and pluck it.
- Be prepared to make love to her once she departs the bath. If she was not in the mood prior to the bath she may very well be upon leaving it and don't deny her. But again I caution you not to expect sex when she is done or even hint at this being your ultimate goal. But be prepared for fireworks if you do it right.
- Make no noise while she is in the bath. Find a book and read. Noises can break her mood and relaxation and possibly even scare her a bit.
- Make sure you do all of the cleanup following the bath.
- Do not interrupt her for any reason. Lock the kids in their room if you have to. Kids these days want to be in their room anyway, playing video games or what not.

- Make sure the tub is spotlessly clean before drawing the bath.
- Make sure there is a bath mat next to the tub. Bubble bath products can be very slick and having your lady slip and injure herself will not produce the desired effect you had intended.

Show Her That You Are Romantic...

The Collage or Scrap Book

The following is a listing of potential small and big romantic ideas for your lady. This listing is for the most part self explanatory, but could also be used to spark new ideas for your lady. Not all will suit every lady, so be cautious in their application and try always to pick ones that she will enjoy as opposed to only those things that you want to do. Many of these ideas came from ladies and so refer to the list often as I do myself. Just because I compiled these ideas does not mean that I have them memorized.

When you first begin dating a lady or even after some years of marriage consider this effort every six months or a year or whatever time period seems appropriate.

The dictionary defines "collage" as "An artistic composition of materials and objects pasted over a surface...". I thought I might put this in for many of us men folk who don't know the term.

For the period of time you have chosen, keep all receipts (cut off the price tag...she knows what you spent on the meal), ticket stubs from events or movies you have seen, a flower petal from each time you have given her flowers, programs from events, photographs, etc. Virtually anything flat will do. Place or glue these items on a flat piece of heavy card board or similar surface in the best artistic manner you can muster (it won't really matter).

Fill in the blank spaces (if any) with words cut from a magazine. (Buy one **Cosmopolitan Magazine** and you will have all the words you ever need for many collages). These words should be things like "Love, commitment, sugar, sweet, friendship, honey, long term, memories, long lasting, living, honor, etc. Put in what you feel.

Have the composition framed nicely under glass, put the appropriate dates on the back and present it to your lady.

You can also accomplish this task with a scrap book which contains plastic insert pages and pockets. Get one of good quality that a woman would appreciate and place memorabilia in it on a regular basis.

Love Notes

Write love notes and leave them laying around the house for her to find. These notes do not have to be elaborate or lengthy. The fact that you do it for her is worth more than their content. You can also place these notes in her car or in her purse (Better be on top. I sincerely believe to this day that Jimmy Hoffa will someday be found in the bottom of my lady friend's purse).

You could also stop by her place of employment and leave her notes, but place it not in view but someplace where she will find it soon. Put a date on it if you like.

The Message on the Mirror

Find something with which you can write her a note on the bathroom mirror. This is especially good if you leave for work before her. This will then likely be what greets her first in the morning and can set the tone for the whole day. Bar soap works, but do not use anything that will be permanent or you will end up buying a new mirror. Sticky notes will also do quite nicely.

If she sometimes uses very hot water from the lavatory, write the note so that it only becomes visible when the mirror steams up. This trick can also work at the kitchen sink if there is a window behind it.

Rent a Billboard

This may not be economically feasible, but you might be surprised how little the cost is in certain locations. Look for a blank billboard on a route she usually travels or in a location where you can "just happen" to be traveling by. The message can be simple and in one color and the billboard rented for just one day potentially. If the billboard owner does not currently have it rented he will most likely appreciate a little extra income from it and can suggest who will make and post the message.

Have Wine Made in Her Name

In many parts of the country there are now wineries which can produce small quantities of quite delicious wines with your choice of label. Pick one out you think she would like and use her name in a creative way for the label. Buy a sufficient quantity so that it can be served at dinner parties in the future. It is, of course, hoped that you will be present at these future dinners and have not done something to make her wish to drink alone.

Send Her Love Letters

Almost no one sends letters any more. I know...I know; everyone uses the internet and e-mail. Do it anyway and hand write it. Call me old fashion and a dinosaur, but a good love letter on good stationary seems more personal and is certainly more permanent and romantic. If you are a lousy writer then check out some poetry books and steal their expressions of love. Use every six bit word you can find, unless, of course, your lady didn't get beyond the sixth grade. At least attempt to show her that you are smart even if she knows better.

Sing to Her if You Can or Play an Instrument

I can not carry a tune with handles on it, and I blackmail eight Karaoke Bars to pay me $10.00 a week not to sing, in that I can clear out a whole bar in less than half a song. But if you can sing then pick out a special love song and sing it for your lady in the appropriate setting. Also, if you play an instrument, do it just for her.

And if You Can't

You may consider hiring a barbershop group or small glee club group to appear at her residence and sing to her on your behalf. Make it early in the evening, maybe just prior to a scheduled date. Don't worry about the neighbors. The nearby women will love it and likely give some grief to their mates for not ever having done likewise.

Dance with Her

It doesn't matter what time of the day it is or what the setting. If you hear music and the two of you are alone, then grab your lady and dance with her. I am not talking about a Foxtrot or Waltz, just cuddle her and shuffle your feet. Ladies constantly complain about their men's reluctance to dance in public places, so dance with her in private. Also consider taking ballroom dance classes with your lady. Having taken them myself, I can assure you that a man who dances well is in great demand. You will never lack for feminine companionship in any public place for dancing.

If You Have Any Artistic Ability

Try sketching or painting a nice flower or other motif on an appropriate part of your lady's anatomy. You should use only water based pen markers or paint so that she can wash it off. The location of this should not be sexual. I like doing it on a knee. It is sensual, but not too much so.

The Travel Map

If you and your lady travel frequently or plan on doing so, secure a map and mark the places you have been and the places you intend to go someday. Frame it (not under glass) and update it as necessary.

This is what dreams are made of and you want your lady to have pleasant dreams.

Champagne and Strawberries

This can be a used as a means for ending a date, an addition to the bubble bath described herein, a dessert for a meal you have cooked for her, or an addition to a home rented movie. If your lady does not drink alcohol, then purchase a non-alcoholic substitute. There is something about the combination of the bubbly taste of Champagne and the sweetness of strawberries which evokes sensuous sentiments.

A Portrait of Your Lady

Either commission a sketch or portrait of your lady, have a pleasing caricature done at an arts festival, or at the very least get a blow up photograph nicely framed. You may also consider having a "Glamour Shot" done of her at the local Mall.

Breakfast in Bed

This suggestion is obviously for the married men among you. If and when you do it, pay attention to the details and have the right equipment for service in bed. Try to always include a flower and a love note, serve the breakfast to her and then depart the room. Eating in bed can sometimes be a messy affair.

A Midnight Breakfast

At the conclusion of a date some evening, either at her place or yours, prepare a midnight breakfast. If at her place have all of the ingredients with you. The menu can, of course, depart somewhat from bacon and eggs. Consider fruits and a light omelet with spinach and mushrooms; whatever you know she will like. A little Champagne can also be appropriate. Nothing spicy or heavy which can impact sleep.

Make Something for Her

Regardless of the skill set you have (woodworking, metal craft, artistic ability, etc.) make something permanent for your lady. It doesn't even have to be that well made as long as it shows effort and care. Something personal and in tune with her likes is recommended, but just do it.

Personal Ads in the Paper

Place a notice in the personal section of your local newspaper praising her and expressing your love. Do not use anything but her first name and purchase extra copies of the newspaper for keepsakes.

Fix Something for Her

Whether married or not, living together or not, a lady will always have something that is broken or a project that needs to be done. It can be as simple as getting the squeak out of a door, or as extensive as repairing a broken down section of fence. Rest assured there will be something that she needs done, so find it and either fix it or find out how to do it. Also consider the new item she wants. It may be just an additional shelf in the laundry room or her closet, but show her that you are both willing and a handy man. After all, the comedian Tim Allen said his mother considered men to only be necessary for lawn care and vehicle maintenance. (More about this in the Not so Romantic Section of this Book)

Relive an Experience with Her Father

Through conversation try and discover a pleasurable experience your lady had with her father then attempt to reproduce this experience with you. It might have been a trip, an outing, or just a dinner. Most, but not all ladies can point to a time or instance where they were especially close to their father. Do not attempt this if your lady was not close to her Dad or he has passed recently. It could thus be painful for her.

Write Her a Poem

Just try and come up with something that rhymes and displays your true sentiments about her. She will appreciate the effort and the time you spent even if your poetry is lousy.

Read Poetry to Her

So you are a lousy poet and have trouble expressing your feelings adequately. Try reading Browning or Whitman to her. Even though the words are from someone else, you reading them to her convey a sense that they are your words too. Allow her to savor the words and at least fantasize that they are also yours.

Lounge in Front of the Fireplace

In cold weather, and if you have a fireplace, strike it up for you and your lady. Have some soft music playing, plenty of pillows on the floor along with a suitable beverage and just lounge in front of the fire. Stoking this fire could stoke the fires of her heart. If you do not have a fireplace then try a campfire in a suitable location, preferably a beach, but even a backyard will do. (Check the fire ordinances for your neighborhood or city first)

Never Stop Learning About Your Lady

In the movie **Fireproof,** the **Love Dare** book admonishes us men to continually learn about our lady. It effectively states that most men will only have the equivalence of a high school diploma at the time of marriage, but we should endeavor to seek a college degree, then a masters and onward to a PhD when it comes to knowledge of our lady. She will indeed change with time, but never stop seeking out her likes, dislikes, and the true essence of her soul. It is a journey well worth taking and will hold many fascinations and rewards.

The Second Wedding

This is sometimes called a reaffirmation of vows. This can be done at almost any time, but it usually occurs on a milestone anniversary, like the 10th or 25th. It can be elaborate or simple, but reaffirming your vows before a minister and possibly witnesses can be very powerful. You are telling your lady that you would marry her all over again. It is also important that you hear the vows again and contemplate their deepest meaning. The date of this second wedding does not have to be an anniversary.

Post the Marriage Vows

Print up your marriage vows in large type. This can be done on most computers. Frame them and hang in a conspicuous place in the house like your bedroom. Then more importantly read them on occasion.

The Surprise Party

For her birthday or any other suitable occasion, throw her a surprise party. Do all of the coordination, but enlist the help of her friends and/or family. Make sure that you get a complete list of her friends. Excluding even one could make that friend of hers an enemy for both of you. Remember that if it is a birthday event, no jokes from you about her age. Her girl friends can do that, but not you!

The Luxury Car Rental

Try renting a luxury car for a weekend just for your lady to ride around in. This does, of course, assume that she does not already have one. Do not drive the rental car yourself. Allow her the pleasure.

The Words "I Love You" are Just a Start

While many learned sources indicate that you should say "I Love You" at least seven times per day to your lady, allow me to offer some thoughts on this matter. I agree with the seven times, but I also recommend that the words be spoken not just in response to her having said them to you. Beat her to the punch. If you love her **SAY IT** often. These words are very important to women. It is okay to show her that you love her, but never forget to say the words too. I also recommend that you add certain other phrases such as "I cherish you", "I adore you", "I value you", "I desire you", "I need you", "You are the love of my life", "You are everything I need", "You make my life complete", "You are my better half", etc. Every woman needs to hear these words from her man.

Dinner for Her Parents

Either take her parents out to dinner or better yet arrange for them to go to dinner together on you. This can be done with a gift certificate or just leaving a credit card with the management. The effort you make should be combined with a card to the parents which thanks them for raising such a wonderful lady.

The Tribute

Get a very large greeting card or small diary book and ask her friends and/or family to write tributes to her. This is similar to the type of thing you see in senior year high school year books. Present it to her at a gathering of her friends or in private depending on the nature of the tributes given. Use your best judgment.

Dedicate a Song on the Radio

Not many radio stations do this any more, but if you can arrange it then try this. Call a local station late at night. You will most often be connected with the DJ on duty and make the request. Make sure you are both listening to the station.

The Calendar of Events

Purchase a large calendar with blank spaces and detail all of the events you have had over the past year. Also consider a calendar for the coming year which outlines special dates (her birthday, etc.) and things you hope to do with her.

Gift from a Trip

If you are a man who travels as a result of business, you may grease the skids from your absences by remembering to bring your lady something from the places you have been. I do not mean a T-Shirt, unless, of course your lady really likes them. Find something that is a local product and bring it back to her. Or better yet, whenever possible, try and take your lady along on some trips. Just be sure that you are able to spend some time with her during the course of the trip. Do not spend all your trip time in meetings and business dinners.

Enroll Your Lady in a Class

In the course of your journey of discovery with your lady, you will possibly hear her say that she has always wanted to take art lessons or learn how to ride horses, or take ballroom dancing classes. If you have the financial means and she has the time, then surprise her with at least an introductory lesson in her choice of pursuits. Do not enroll her in a long term commitment. She may discover that she really doesn't like what she once thought might be fun. So do not commit her for any length of time. For something like ballroom dancing then you enroll with her, otherwise enroll her in a class as a special thing just for her.

Buy Her Some Stock

Depending on your pocketbook, consider buying her some shares in a stock. This can range from a "penny stock" or one listed on the

New York Stock Exchange. Try and make it a stock that will grow and is with a company in which she has some interest.

The Airplane Banner

Proclaim your love through an airplane banner at a time and place where she will see it. This is somewhat expensive, but could be a very memorable moment for her. It is certainly less cost than the idea that one woman had; "Take your lady to Italy one night for dinner."

The Only Thing I Will Say About Sex

Why do female Black Widow spiders kill the male after mating? To stop the snoring before it starts!

For those you who are married I will humbly offer only one piece of advice on sex. The bedroom is not the only place to enjoy sex. Try some variety in your locations to keep it fresh and exciting for your lady. Other venues may not be as comfortable, but they can frequently be more memorable.

The First Kiss and Some Thoughts on Doing it Right

While this book should in no way be construed as a sex manual, a proper chaste first kiss is important to a lady. Upon returning from a first date a woman's friends will frequently make one of their questions to her "Did he kiss you and is he a good kisser?" I am talking here about the first kiss which is frequently a life time memory for many women. First and foremost, do not force a kiss on a lady on the first date. You may offer it, but graciously accept a refusal and try again if you have a second date. A refusal on her part does not necessarily mean she has no interest in you.

To do it right I offer the following suggestions; Grasp her face gently by placing your hands flat on each side of her face, then following that first gentle kiss on the lips, kiss her on the forehead and then possibly kiss her eyes. She will close them for you, but in case she doesn't, do not lick her open eyes. (Some ladies expressed concern about the kiss on the eyes, effectively saying it was too intimate for a first kiss. I tend to agree, so save this one for the second date or second kiss or when you feel it might be appropriate). Hands on her face will express tenderness and keep the lady from worrying about what else they may be trying to touch.

If you do it right you may then be seriously kissed back and in a more passionate manner. Be a good kisser for your lady for all of your time together.

For the first kiss make sure you keep your tongue to yourself.

If with her first kiss to you she sticks her tongue half way down your throat you may want to consider a second more passionate kiss back or perhaps additional action on your part, but don't push it too far.

Back in the days before the automatic car unlocking mechanisms we enjoy today, a friend of mine stated that it was a very good sign if a lady reached over to unlock your door after you seated her. He went on to say that if she straddled the console it was a better sign, but if she immediately jumped in the back seat...don't even bother to start the car.

Show Her Friends, Her Family, and Your Children That You Are Romantic...

It is frequently important to a lady who has an interest in you that members of her family, her friends and co-workers also express their approval. She may say that she doesn't care what they think, but trust me...she does. Having their approval or disapproval may not be a deal breaker or relationship ender, but their opinion of you can help make the embers in your lady's heart turn into a roaring fire.

For the most part, if you do the things contained in this book; always acting like a gentleman, being honest, and just showing common courtesy, you will receive the approval that you seek and need. I would, however, like to offer some suggestions.

For Members of Her Family

A friend of mine in Texas offered the advice, when I mentioned meeting the family of a lady for the first time, to have a "conceal and carry permit" which allows you to carry a concealed firearm on your person. I hope this won't be necessary, at least until they get to know you better. This worldly piece of counsel aside.

Do not shy away from meeting them. Be courteous, friendly and show interest in your lady. Seek out their interests and try to find common ground for conversation. Listen to them. They may be, at first, suspicious and somewhat cold toward you. Don't let it bother you. Just continue to be kind and respectful.

At the proper time ask them to join you and your lady for a restaurant dinner and pick up the check. Include them in other activities which may be appropriate. Be kind and respectful to your lady and eventually they will be kind to you. Your lady is their relative so they want to be protective of her. Earn their trust.

Meeting the Father/Mother for the First Date

If your date resides at home you will most likely encounter their mother/father or both at the front door. Be polite and respectful, and above all <u>talk</u> to them. My father, upon meeting some of my friends when I was in high school, was always suspicious of any of my friends who did not talk to him. He was very wise, because those friends of mine who were quiet were the very same ones with whom I go into trouble and mischief.

I do hope, however, you do not have the same encounter I once had upon picking up a girl for the first date. Her 6'-10", 300 lb. father met me at the door and asked me if my intentions toward his daughter were honorable or dishonorable. I gulped, as I stared skyward up to him, and asked if I had a choice? He did not appreciate the intended humor. All of you men who have dating age daughters can understand what I am saying. I am both sad and glad that I fathered no daughters, although one of my friends whose daughter was arriving at the dating age remarked that he had no trepidations regarding his daughter's coming of age. He simply stated "I am not worried. I will just have her spayed and turn her out." He was, of course, just kidding.

For Her Friends

All of the above applies equally to your lady's friends. In some cases this is even more so, since her friends may be closer to her than members of her own family. A lady friend once told me that her family was dysfunctional. I then asked her to name one that wasn't. You may be courting your lady, but always remember that her friends and family have known her before you came along.

Co-Workers

For a full time working woman, it is quite possible that she will be spending more time with them than with you. Give them respect and be courteous, especially to any bosses she may have even if they are the "boss from hell".

Try one or more of these ideas for the office:

- Bring donuts to the office one morning, at least a dozen or two.
- Bring pizzas to the office for lunch one day. Do it early and warn your lady that you are doing it so she can prompt people what is coming.
- Stop by the office early one day before she arrives and drop off an apple, a single flower or greeting card for your lady. Her female co-workers will be envious.
- Take your lady to lunch from work and try sometimes to surprise her, if possible.
- Take them all out (As many as you can afford, but don't offend anyone) for a happy hour drink after work one day.
- In as many ways as possible show your lady's co-workers that you are romantic. Do not, however, call her excessively at her place of employment. It could cause considerable problems for her and even result in termination.

Your Children

Showing respect, love and romance for your lady in front of your children is very important for family harmony and the future of your children.

A man who displays these characteristics in front of his son is paving the way for him to have respect for the girls he will encounter, while instructing the boy in how to woo a young lady. Likewise a man who romances and loves his wife will demonstrate to his daughter that she should rightfully expect similar treatment from the boys who enter her life, thus making her prone to the right choices amongst boys.

Also never forget the old adage that when Momma is not happy no one is.

Not So Romantic (But Do It Anyway)...

How does a woman keep a man from reading her e-mail?
Title her mail folder "Instruction Manual"!

Being a romantic guy to your lady does not always involve grand gestures or moonlight walks. Being romantic is frequently about little things which show that you care and her value to you, so don't neglect the small stuff. Some examples might be:

- Vehicle Maintenance – Check on your lady's car. While some women may be inclined to do this, it is generally not high on their priority list. Check the fluid levels (Oil, power steering fluid, window washing liquid, etc.), the tire pressure, oil change timelines, etc. Also sometimes fill up the tank for your lady. These efforts could also save you financial headaches at a later time.
- Take note of the inspection and registration stickers on your lady's car and renew when needed for her.
- Automobile Washing – Wash her car for her and vacuum it out, or possibly have it detailed. She will love you for it.
- Automobile Emergency Gear – Place a can of automatic tire inflation foam in her car along with other emergency gear like flares, flashlight, etc.
- Check out That Noise – If your lady hears a noise in the house go check it out **always**. It may be a useless exercise to you, but just do it for her peace of mind.

- Take out the Trash – When she asks you to and when she doesn't. It is a scientific fact that the female nose is more sensitive than a man's. So get off the couch Mr. Potato and go do it, especially if it is dark outside. Also, always replace the bag in the container immediately.
- Bring in the mail. She may, however, not want you to do so. She may want that credit card offer from Macy's or want to prevent you from seeing that she already has one.
- Change the batteries in the fire alarms.
- Always walk around the house at night to insure that all windows are closed and all doors are locked.
- Change the filters in the home air conditioner system (Could also save you a costly repair bill in the future)
- Do Some Every Day Chores – One of the most common complaints by married women, those who work outside of the house, and those who don't is that they typically do 80% to 90% of the household chores. Guys…give her a break. Get off your backsides and help her out. You know what needs to be done, even though we men folk are infamous for feigning ignorance of these tasks. Allow me to list just a few so that you can no longer wear the male mantle of stupidity. Cooking the meals, washing the dishes, grocery shopping, doing the laundry, vacuuming or scrubbing the floors, cleaning the tub, toilet; sink, kitchen, etc., running to the dry cleaner, dusting and the most common overwhelming task a woman faces is **picking up after her man**. Add children to the mix and all of this becomes much worse. So allow me to offer some suggestions on little ways which may help us slovenly men to help our ladies. **(I have been cautioned to explain that most men should not attempt to wash a woman's delicate laundry… ask her if you don't know what these items are).**
- The Little Things Which Help – This listing is some little things that a man can do without much effort and which can save time around the house for both her and you.

- Keep a hand towel by the bathroom sink and wipe down the counter and mirror after use.
- After using the toilet grab some toilet paper and wipe down the rim (we men do splatter and we can't help it. Sorry ladies)
- Go buy lots of trash baskets (They are cheap) and place wherever you might have to throw something away. (i.e. dry cleaning tag, old razors, dryer lint filter, etc.) We need to have something close by, otherwise we might wear ourselves out taking a few steps.
- **How many men does it take to change a roll of toilet paper?** No one knows it has never been done. Place extra toilet paper rolls next to the toilet or on the tank so that you can reload while reading your "Sports Illustrated".
- Get numerous laundry baskets and divide up your dirty clothes as you take them off. I suggest two for washing (one for colors and one for whites) and one for dry cleaning.
- Unroll your socks when removing them. They do not come clean if rolled up.
- Get a rack of some sort for sweaty wet clothes so that they will dry before placing them in the proper basket. Do not put sweaty wet clothes in a basket with other clothes.
- Walk your dirty dishes and glasses from the table to the sink, even if you are not doing the washing. Empty the excess food into the garbage and rinse them off. Also place them in the dishwasher, but not if the dishes there are clean.
- Take a fresh glass or plate out of the dishwasher in lieu of the cabinet. You are at least helping to unload the dishwasher. (Better yet, if the dishes are clean, put the dishes back in the cabinet)

- Use paper cups and/or plates whenever possible then throw them away.
- When departing work and your wife is at home, call her to see if she needs anything you can pick up on the way home.
- When sitting down for your favorite TV show, do something which is not a distraction. (i.e. sharpen the kitchen knives for her, polish some silverware, sort some socks from the laundry, fold some towels, sort the mail, fill up the salt and pepper shakers, dust the coffee table, etc.) It is very doubtful that you will miss anything on the tube.
- When you move about the house, just look for things that need to be picked up or thrown away and carry them with you to the proper place.
- When you reach for a paper towel to dry your hands wipe something down like a counter, etc.

- Illness – If your lady becomes sick try and cater to her every need. Get her over the counter remedies, fill her prescriptions, take her to the doctor, cook for her, run errands for her and see that she is comfortable. "In sickness and in health" is a serious thing in any relationship.
- Walk the Dog – If you have a dog then it needs walking. Do not ask your lady to walk a dog especially at night.
- Wash the Dog – Just do it and often.
- Yard Work – If she has a house try doing some yard work for her. Even if she has a lawn service, there will still be things you can do like weeding beds, trimming bushes, etc.
- Kill the Bugs – Most ladies have an aversion to bugs. Kill them for her when they are seen and promptly dispose of them.
- Personal Protection – Give your lady a container of mace or a stun gun for her personal protection and show her how to use it.

- Pet Peeves – Figure out that thing you do constantly which irks her and resolve not to do it for a day, week, month or whatever. If she notices, fine, but if she does not notice, then keep refraining from doing it until she does notice.
- List Maker – Be a list maker when planning a trip, an event, a party, etc. Put together this list even if your lady does likewise. Comparing the lists can be helpful and also reduce stress of your lady.
- Gratitude – Besides saying thank you to your lady whenever she does something for you, try every day to make a point of showing your special appreciation for something she has done for you. A little extra over and above the thank you.

How many men does it take to tile a bathroom? Only one if you slice him real thin!
(I just thought this one was funny)

Dates (Beyond dinner and a movie)...

Don't get me wrong; dinner and a movie are a great opening date. The dinner is a time for good conversation and getting to know each other, and the movie can be a good time for first holding hands and suspend the need for conversation which may be difficult on the first date. Guys, make that first movie a romantic comedy, not a slasher or skin flick

While dinner and a movie are a fine opening, do not put your lady's feet to sleep with the same venue every Friday or Saturday night. Ladies typically like excitement and variety. Show her that you can be both original and someone who will challenge her senses and intellect.

Please understand that the following suggestions are not just for first dates, third dates or the 1000th date. Married men should also try to vary the routine. The point being that there should not be a routine.

Allow me to make some suggestions on possible dates which may or may not be possible, economically feasible or even desirable for all couples. These are just possibilities which you may not have considered. Remember to take a camera for many of these dates.

- **Amusement Park** – There are things to do for all ages at an amusement park. They are not just for the young and can make the old feel young at heart. It also a documented fact that the adrenaline produced in scary rides is similar to feelings evoked by love. If there are arcade games then try very hard to win something for her, even if it very small. It could become a cherished keepsake for her.

- **Landing Planes** - Take her to an airport one evening and park where the planes are landing. Have the appropriate beverage and snacks and use this time for serious conversation and getting to know one another's aspirations and dreams for the future. You may also title the evening as one where you talk of future travel desires.

- **Wine and Cheese** – Have a wine and cheese evening. In addition to wine and cheese you can also get whatever else in finger foods that might be desirable. Feed her from your hand at times. This makes for a relaxing evening without a more formal dinner. You may also, as part of the evening, visit a good wine store with your lady and jointly seek the advice of the store's expert on wines. Guys, don't forget the cork puller and don't buy a wine which does not require one.

- **Sunset Viewing** – In virtually all locations there is some place from which viewing a sunset is especially attractive. Find this location, try to pick an evening with some clouds so that God paints a spectacular picture, take the appropriate beverages and seating and just sit back relax and enjoy. Be prepared to take photos and include your lady in some of them. Also consider watching a sunrise.

- **Walk in the Rain** – Have the rain gear and umbrella, but take your lady for a short walk in a warm gentle rain. It makes for good close contact under the single umbrella and the worst that can ensue is that you get a little wet.

- **A Walk on the Beach** – If you are fortunate enough to live near the ocean, then a moonlight walk on the beach can melt a lady's heart. But even a lake will do if you are inland. Make sure to bring a water container, wine skin, or other beverage. Also make sure that your lady is suitably clothed for warmth and has on the appropriate shoes.

- **Small Plane or Balloon Ride** – Arrange for a small plane ride at night or an early morning balloon ride. In most places this can be arranged either through charter services or at a local flying service. Many chartered balloon rides include Champagne as part of the trip. Otherwise take it with you. A night time small plane ride is best. The lights are spectacular and there is usually very little turbulence, which can be scary to some. As a pilot I know this to be true. I once took a date in college up in a plane ride at night with another couple. I asked the young lady if anyone had ever taken her this close to the stars. The other guy told the rest of the fraternity about my line, and I caught ribbing from my fraternity brothers for weeks. Please skip the cheesy line that I used. You can also consider the idea of a glider plane ride although you may not be able to do this together.

- **Winter Retreat** – In the dead of winter when it is cold, rainy or snowing and if you do not own a hot tub or sauna, then rent a hotel room that does and stay a day or night with your lady. Depending on the status of your relationship, the hot tub experience could be in swimsuits during the day, but should be appreciated by your lady. If she does not like how she looks in a swimsuit then allow her to enter and exit the tub when you are not present. Use your judgment as to whether or not this will be pleasurable for your lady or make her uncomfortable. If you are married go for it all the way. Have some bubbly available, along with candles, etc. (See bubble bath section herein)

- **Live Sporting Event** – Even if your lady has no interest in sports try taking her to a live event. There is considerable excitement at most live events, and she will likely get caught up in the experience even if she wants to know what inning it is at a football game. Now with the price of tickets these days, you might consider just dropping in on the local high school game. It may be just as much fun for her as an NFL game.

- **Progressive Dinner** – Allow me to define "Progressive Dinner" in that I only learned recently what this means. Take her to one restaurant for an appetizer, and then depart to another for the main course, followed by a third venue for the dessert course. Try and finish up at still another which has music for dancing. One young lady also suggested that for this evening rent an expensive sports car to travel from location to location.

- **The Limo Pick Up** – Instead of picking her up yourself for a date one night, have a licensed limo driver pick her up and bring her to the restaurant where you meet her. In other words give her the movie star treatment. It may make her feel like she is on her prom night all over again. Be sure to have the limo driver call you when he arrives at her place so that you then call her about it. This is for her safety and peace of mind. She may not want to enter the car of a stranger, even a limo.

- **Homage to "9-1/2 Weeks"** – In this movie the man (Mickey Rourke) sits the lady (Kim Basinger) down in the kitchen, blindfolds her and proceeds to feed her various foods, which are cold, hot, spicy, unusual, or sensual. Use your imagination. You are taking your lady on a sensual taste trip.

- **Cultural Events** – Even if your lady is a tee shirt and blue jeans type of girl, try including an occasional cultural date which can be any or all of the following: Symphony, Opera, Arts Museum, Touring Broadway Show, etc. She will have the opportunity to dress up and you will benefit from her doing so. Try and be knowledgeable about the event you are taking her to and by all means give her plenty of warning about the event. She may need a dress, hairdo, etc. If she is a blue jeans type then suggest various possibilities to her and gauge her reaction.

- **Charity Event** – There are numerous charities which host balls, dinners and other types of fund raisers on a frequent basis. Try and discover a particular charity which interests her (i.e. SPCA, Breast Cancer, etc.) and then take her to the fundraiser and try and make a contribution when you are there. It will show that you have a giving and generous spirit, which most ladies want in a man.

- **Charitable Activity** – Try participating in a charitable event together. This could mean 5K run or walk, or many other types of events.

- **Hiking or Camping Trip** – If your lady is the outdoor type, then you will soon discover what she likes. If not, then just a hike around a city park will suffice. It is good exercise and a good time for serious conversation. Never underestimate the value of conversation with a lady. As for camping she must be truly an outdoor kind of lady and you need to have some camping skills to pull this one off. Not having outdoor skills can make this type of date a disaster. I once took a lady on a camping trip, forgot the toilet paper, burned the food and pitched the tent under a screech owl that screeched all night long. She obviously remembered the date, but chose to forget me from that time on.

- **The Picnic** – Having grown up in the south a picnic for me has meant a feast for the flies, ants and other bugs. I do, however, understand that not all parts of the country have these problems. For some reason many ladies like a picnic or at least the idea of it. If you choose to ask her on one, please plan carefully. Check the weather carefully and choose the location wisely. Then make a list of all of the required items which are in addition to the food and beverages. Remember to bring napkins (cloth preferably), wet wipes, cups, plates, and other containers which will not blow away in the breeze, ice chest, a table cloth, and any other amenities you can think of. Also check for the availability of nearby toilet facilities. Include bug spray and sun block.

- **The Alternate Picnic** – Find a park with a gazebo or a location with good picnic tables. Set a table cloth with good quality dishes, flatware, glasses, etc. Have a flower in a vase, a boom box with good music and a meal in containers which can be plated easily. The food should be selections which are served cold. (i.e. Potato salad, green salads, cold cuts, etc.) This accomplishes the outdoor setting requirement, but helps defeat the other elements. You can also try what I call the European lunch which includes wine, cheese, summer sausage and bread.

- **The Concert** – Find out who her favorite recording artist is, then investigate when and where this artist will be appearing live. Then depending upon your financial ability, make every effort to take her to see this artist even if it means flying the both of you to another city. Surprise will work best if you can arrange it.

- **The Rental Movie** – For an easy going date, rent a movie she will like, but don't stop there. Get some popcorn and melt some butter for it. Also provide a wide arrangement of typical movie fare (i.e. Goobers, Malted Milk Balls, Pickles, etc.). Then offer her the selection. Be sure to lower the lights to simulate the movie experience as much as possible. Cuddle her or at least hold her hand.

- **Get Her Dirty** – Only for some ladies! Take her on an adventure or date in which she will get absolutely dirty. This could be to a local park in the rain where you both slip and slide in the mud or many other scenarios. Make sure you have fresh water and towels with which to clean up a bit before entering the car, and also have covers for your car seats. Women at almost all ages are much cleaner than us men, but for some they might perceive the opportunity to get really dirty as exciting.

- **Fishing** – More men fish than ladies, but if you bait the hook, cast the line or just provide a cane pole, this type date can be a good opportunity for conversation. Try, however, to pick a spot where she is likely to catch something. Even if she has never fished before, carefully observe the delight on her face upon her first catch. I do not recommend a serious fishing expedition unless she is a seasoned fishing veteran. She is unlikely to understand the nuances of remaining still and quiet, and besides, you will defeat the purpose of the date. Also consider your lady's sensibilities when catching fish. You may want to catch and release if she is squeamish.

- **The Project** – Pick a project that the two of you can do together either in a day or over a weekend. Some suggestions might be to plant a garden, plant some rose bushes, etc. The project should be of a creative nature and be something you both can do.

- **Church** – Take your lady to church. There can be spiritual refreshment and you may also hear a message which brings the two of you closer together. Relationships are hard enough to keep together. Godly principles will many times make the difference for a lasting union.

- **Horseback Riding or Horse Event** – Take her on a horse riding trip. Use judgment and caution here. If your lady is not a rider, then you need to rent horses from a stable which specializes in gentle nags (A horse…hopefully not your lady) who will move slowly. If your lady is a cowgirl then find a place for more advanced riding. Also consider a horse event like dressage or exhibition riding. Check out a rodeo or even horse racing. A $2.00 long shot bet which comes in as a winner can provide some real excitement for a day or an evening for your lady. But it doesn't really matter if she wins or not. (I once bet on a horse that went off at 30 to 1. It didn't cross the finish line til a quarter after 2.) Most ladies like horses, so check it out.

- **Trail Ride at a Dude Ranch** – This venue can be found in many places across the country, but check with your lady first. She may have a fear of horses.

- **Train Ride** – While this is not available in many areas, check into it. A long train trip (A few hours) can be wonderfully romantic, especially for a lady who has never been on a train. A trip on the subway in New York or Boston does not qualify unless you are a tourist.

- **Water Activities** – Water, lights, and moonlight are always a winner. Even in arid locations you may be able to find a paddleboat trip on a lake, a dinner trip on a larger boat, or a walk on the beach. If near a coast try the moonlight walk. Rent a canoe or rowboat on a calm day on the lake. Make sure, however, that you employ proper boat safety, you know what you are doing and have life vests and safety gear. A trip on a river with gentle rapids can also be a thrill, but again know what you are doing and check out the river with a prior trip. My canoe trip with my ex wife was not good when I failed to check out a rapid before going into it and she ended up in the water.

- **City Lights** – Take her to a revolving restaurant or at least a venue that is high up in a city and offers a view of city lights at night.

- **Speed** – Fast cars, fast boats, and fast go carts. Never under estimate the value of a thrill for your lady. This is, of course, highly dependent on her age and sense of adventure. You don't want to scare the daylights out of her by doing 90 MPH on a busy side street. Some speed under controlled conditions and with proper safety can exhilarate her immensely. Try the local Go-Cart track. It has plenty of speed when you are that low to the ground and is mostly safe. Do not, however, race against her. Send her out on the track by herself.

- **The Athletic Activity** – Depending again on age and the interests of your lady, consider going skating, biking, or even to the gym together. Women frequently like to observe men in physical activity. It emphasizes manly muscles (assuming you have some) and shows that you are interested in looking good for her. Always ask your lady for any athletic activity before hand. Do not surprise her with this. She may not be physically able to do some things or have a fear of looking awkward.

- **The Long Walk** – Take a long walk together with your lady. It is quiet time, good exercise, and allows for good conversation. For many ladies their schedules would only allow them to walk at night, which is very risky for them to do alone. Be the man and protector and take these walks with her. Consider also the mall walk, which simply means brisk walking in your local mall. It is not dependent on the weather.

- **Bed and Breakfast** – Find the right location and right facility and this can be a terrific getaway and romantic weekend or even one night. Try to choose facilities which do not have all of the modern conveniences (i.e. no television which might tempt you to watch that football game or golf match).

- **The Weekend Getaway** – Especially important for young married couples with small children. As Bill Cosby put it so eloquently, "I am not the boss of my house, but I have seen the boss's job and I don't want it." Dealing with young children day in and out can wither a woman, so find a professional babysitter or trusted relatives and check into a local hotel for even one night. With very young children your lady may not feel comfortable being far away, so make it close, but also a facility where she might receive a relaxing massage or spa treatment. But just getting away for 24 hours can be a real renewal for your lady.

- **The Specialty or Theme Restaurant** – Rather than the same old restaurant dinners check out any specialty restaurants in your area. A Medieval Times theme, magic club, or comedy club can be a real special treat. Comedy can be a great tonic for the mind.

- **Shooting** – Depending again on your lady's sensibilities and assuming that you are knowledgeable, consider a local shooting venue. It can be an indoor range, skeet or trap club, or outdoor range. Most places will rent you the firearms and provide instruction if needed. Just remember that if you ever really hack her off, don't teach her to be a really good shot.

- **The Festival** – Always check the papers for announcements of local or nearby festivals. They can be an arts festival, flower viewing, Irish Fest, etc. This can be an exciting date for both of you.

- **People Watching** – Take your lady to an outdoor romantic location, sit on a park bench or the grass and just watch the people go by. See if you can jointly guess who they are, if they are happy, what they do, etc.

- **The Cruise** – I should contact the cruise lines and ask them for money for what I am about to say. If you can afford it, consider an ocean cruise to be an excellent vacation and an abundantly romantic thing to do for your lady and you. Romance practically oozes from all aspects of a high seas adventure. You can also acquire some very good deals from last minute purchases of a cruise.

- **The Cemetery Walk** – Assuming your lady has experienced no deaths among her family or close friends in the recent past, try going to a very old cemetery and just viewing the headstones. It can be relaxing and historically interesting.

- **The Scavenger or Treasure Hunt** – Thoroughly plan one of these for your lady, with a significant outcome (i.e. A gift she did not expect or a trip you wish to take her on.) Do not make it too difficult, but make it a fun and exciting experience for her.

- **Slumming** – For one date in a long term relationship ask your lady to dress up, (Cocktail dress, but not evening wear) without telling her where you are going. Then take her to some really slummy type, but safe places. (i.e. The jazz club, pool hall, etc.) She will always be the best dressed lady in the place. Under no circumstances do the opposite. Do not take your lady to a fancy place when she is dressed for a casual evening.

- **Photographic Date** – Take your lady to a scenic spot, a formal garden area open to the public, or any outdoor venue. If not using a digital camera, take plenty of film and photograph your lady until she screams for mercy from posing (most won't). Place her so that you see her and the background scenery and shoot away. She will also want some of you, so allow it and/or get a bystander to take a photo of you both.

- **Zoo Trip** – Not just for kids. Try it. Your lady may really enjoy it, and it is good exercise walking around a zoo. Try to do it on a cool day when the odors of the animal are not so pungent.

- **The Circus** – Also not just for kids. Look for when one comes to your town.

- **The Carriage Ride** – Many metropolitan areas have horse drawn carriage or buggy rides around parks and scenic sites. This can be done by day or night. Due, however, to the fact that most of the horse manure is now caught by a bag, I would suggest doing this only on cool or cold days where the odor is not so pervasive. Bring a blanket and snuggle with her.

- **Bird Watching** – Get an Audubon's Guide to Birds, a pair of binoculars (Two would be better) and take your lady to a wildlife place to see how many birds you can spot and identify.

- **Miniature Golf** – A very popular first date for young teens. Try it again, and you and your lady can both feel young.

- **Arcade** – An arcade experience can also be like reliving your early years. Try a place like Dave and Busters, which also caters to adults. A kids arcade can also be fun but you may want to bring ear plugs to dampen the noise from screaming kids.

- **Dog Walk or Park** – If you or your lady has a dog, then consider a visit to a dog park.

- **The Convertible Car** – Rent a nice convertible car for a weekend and drive her around in it. Many women, especially young women love the breeze in their hair. Do not attempt this if your lady has just spent major dollars at her hairdresser. Check the weather.

- **The Planetarium, Arboretum, Etc.** – Visit one of or all of these for a day or evening event.

- **Karaoke** – If your lady sings, by all means take her to a nightclub which offers this. Have her sing often and praise her efforts even if she has a voice like the Wicked Witch of the West.

- **The Library or Music Room** – Spend a few hours at a local library or bookstore browsing and reading books. This assumes that your lady likes to read, but just browsing will provide good topics for conversation. This could also apply to a music room.

- **Skating or Ice Skating Rink** – Even if she is not proficient in either of these, consider it any way. After all you get to help her up if she falls and there can be some great laughs in falling. Always ask your lady about this kind of date first. She may not be able to do this activity and will feel embarrassed about stumbling, or she may not be physically fit enough to do it. She may also have a number of conditions which prevent her from doing it.

- **Go Fly a Kite** – This can be a great experience for an afternoon. Know what you are doing, go to a park or open field and bring refreshments and some snack food, etc.

- **Soda Fountain** – For the elderly and nostalgic among us (Yes I am that old) find an old time soda fountain and take your lady for a delectable treat of a sundae, shake, or whatever.

- **Weenie and Marsh Mellow Roast** – This can be done over a campfire or over the backyard grill, so straighten out some coat hangers and do it right. Smores might also be good.

- **Bike Ride or Tandem Bike** – Rent bikes if you don't already have them or better yet get a tandem bike and have that "bicycle built for two" ride on a good bike trail. Bring water and refreshments.

AND FINALLY...

- **The Date Without You** – In a long term relationship, try sending your lady on a trip with her closest girlfriend. All expenses to be paid for by you. A weekend trip is good, but overnight will also work. At the very least a single night out on the town for their pleasure only. It shows trust on your part, a generous heart, and just may allow you to watch an important game uninterrupted. Don't tell her that and also consider doing it just to show your feelings for her.

Afterword...

It is hoped that this book has been useful to those who have read some or all of it. I am quite certain that many readers will have ideas of their own about what is romantic or not. I am also sure that you may have some unique things of your own to try on your lady. I suggest that you return to the ideas in this book on a frequent basis. I do so myself.

The true point of this book has been to spark some thoughts of things you can do to have a more passionate and exciting relationship with your chosen lady. It is hoped that she will reciprocate in kind with love, romance, care, and kindness, but whether she does or does not, you men as individuals will hopefully be better men for the effort. Love is a chemistry thing and not all ladies will respond to romantic entreaties from a given man. Many other factors are at work.

Try always to use some of the techniques found herein and God will put you together with the woman who will bind with you and complete you as a man.

I believe there is almost nothing so powerful in this world as the love of a woman. I believe that you lucky few men who have experienced it can attest to the often total obsession which a lady can have. As a man whom a lady truly loves, her whole mind, her being, and her soul are completely focused on you. While I believe it is possible that a man can have some of this ecstasy, I do not believe we have the same intensity as that of a woman. I have no scientific data upon which to base this conclusion, but observations tell me it is as I perceive.

I would ask that all men attempt to give as much as you can of yourself in return. Women bring life on to this earth and your special lady can also bring a fuller life to you. Just give in return.

About the Author...

Richard Connelly is a Texas native, who has lived and worked in many places throughout the country. He attended high school in New Orleans and college at Georgia Tech. He is currently single having been married just once with two children.

His career path has been widely varied having worked in construction project management, architecture, real estate appraisal, environmental consulting, real estate market feasibility and development. As he has stated he has no qualifications to write this type of book other than an interest in market survey and statistical analysis. He has interviewed hundreds of individuals over many years to compile the contents of this book. What you will be reading herein is what hundreds of women say is romantic.

He currently works in prison and senior ministries through his church and resides in the Dallas-Ft. Worth area of Texas. Richard is also a licensed pilot and ballroom dancer which has given him many opportunities to seek the opinions of women. He is also the author of a previous book titled **"What Men Really Think About Women...by a Few Good Men"**.